Arya Nair

Arya Nair, a remarkable 17-year-old student currently in the 12th grade at Ryan International School Sharjah. Arya's educational journey began at Smt. Vidyaben D. Gardi High School in Mumbai, where she cultivated her passion for storytelling and laid the groundwork for her impressive academic career.

Not only is Arya an outstanding student, but she is also an emerging author making waves in the literary world. With the recent release of her third book, Facade of Generosity, she continues to captivate readers and expand the beloved Chronicles of the Sisterhood series. Her previous two books have sold out, showcasing her exceptional talent and the deep connection she fosters with her audience.

As she navigates her final year of school, Arya serves as an inspiring example to her peers, demonstrating that with passion and hard work, incredible heights can be achieved. Her journey is a testament to the power of dedication and creativity, and we look forward to seeing where her literary ambitions will take her next.

English Language
Facade of Generosity
(Novel)
by
Arya Nair

♦

Published in October 2024
by Kairali Books Private Limited
Thalikkavu Road, Kannur.
Ph : 0497-2761200
E-Mail : kairalibooksknr@gmail.com

♦

Cover Design
Watermelon

♦

89/24-25/Sl.No.1656/150/NS.18.6
ISBN 978-93-5973-897-0

Facade of Generosity

(It is the Third book in the series, Chronicles of the Sisterhood)

Arya Nair

Kairali Books

Dedicated to my Great Grandmom,
Smt. Saradamma. M.
(May her soul be at peace)

Spotlight

Arya Nair, a remarkable 17-year-old student currently in the 12th grade at Ryan International School Sharjah. Arya's educational journey began at Smt. Vidyaben D. Gardi High School in Mumbai, where she cultivated her passion for storytelling and laid the groundwork for her impressive academic career.

Not only is Arya an outstanding student, but she is also an emerging author making waves in the literary world. With the recent release of her third book, 'Facade of Generosity', she continues to captivate readers and expand the beloved 'Chronicles of the Sisterhood' series. Her previous two books have sold out, showcasing her exceptional talent and the deep connection she fosters with her audience.

As she navigates her final year of school, Arya serves as an inspiring example to her peers, demonstrating that with passion and hard work, incredible heights can be achieved. Her journey is a testament to the power of dedication and creativity, and we look forward to seeing where her literary ambitions will take her next.

Ryan International School Celebrates
Arya Nair's New Book Launch

Sharjah - A wave of pride has once again swept through the hallways of Ryan International School Sharjah, centered around Ms. Arya Nair. With her latest release, Facade of Generosity, Arya adds another remarkable chapter to the Chronicles of the Sisterhood series, exemplifying the exceptional talent nurtured within our educational community.

As Principal, I am continually reaffirmed in my belief in the strength of our education system, the unwavering dedication of our teaching staff, and the boundless potential of our students. Arya's journey not only inspires her peers but also serves as a testament to what passion, perseverance, and creativity can achieve.

I invite all members of our school community to immerse themselves in Arya's work and offer their support. Let us celebrate this significant achievement and rally behind our young author as she ascends new heights in her literary journey. May her words continue to inspire and enlighten, leaving an indelible mark on the literary world.

With Immense Pride
Ms. Daizy Paul
Principal
Ryan International School Sharjah

Chapter 1
Shadows of the Past

Mumbai's skyline shimmered with the promise of new beginnings as Isabella, Sophia, Elena, Amelia, and Olivia stepped out of the bustling Chhatrapati Shivaji Maharaj Terminus. The city, once their childhood playground, now beckoned them as they returned for college after years abroad in Dubai. The familiar chaos of Mumbai traffic, the heady mix of aromas from street vendors, and the vibrant street life greeted them, painting a picture of homecoming.

As the five friends reunited, their excitement was tinged with nostalgia and a sense of unfinished business. They remembered their last visit to India vividly. It was during Elena's sister's wedding—a celebration marred by darkness they could never forget. The joy of the occasion had been overshadowed by the menacing presence of Queen Nickolav, the infamous trafficker who had threatened them with a chilling message: *"Bud't egotovy k Adskomu ognyu!"* *"Get ready for Hellfire!"*

Isabella glanced at her friends, her eyes reflecting a mixture of apprehension and resolve. "Can you believe it's been over a year since we last faced her? It feels like just yesterday we were trying to piece everything together."

Sophia, ever the pragmatic one, nodded. "And yet, the threat still lingers. We dismantled part of her operation, but we know she's still out there. Her influence might have shifted, but it hasn't disappeared."

Elena shivered slightly, recalling the terror of those days. "I keep wondering if we've seen the last of her. What if she's planning something even more sinister?"

Amelia's gaze was steely with determination. "We've come back to Mumbai to start fresh, but we can't ignore the possibility that she might still be a threat. We need to stay vigilant."

Olivia, who had been quiet until now, broke her silence. "Let's not forget why we're here. College is our immediate priority, but we should also keep our eyes open for anything that could lead us back to Nickolav. We can't let our guard down."

As they made their way through the crowded streets of Mumbai, the city seemed to pulsate with energy and secrets. Their arrival had not gone unnoticed. Rumours of their return began to spread quickly, and with them, the shadows of past adversaries stirred.

The echo of that threat had haunted them since, a constant reminder of the danger that lurked in the shadows. Queen Nickolav was known for her ruthlessness - exploiting the vulnerable and engaging in heinous crimes that seemed almost beyond comprehension.

The threat from Queen Nickolav and the injustice perpetrated by the fraudulent trust had ignited a fire within them. They knew their return to Mumbai was not merely a return to old routines but a step into a new chapter filled with challenges and responsibilities.

Their first stop was Isabella's family home. The sight of her parents, who had come to pick them up, was like a balm to her soul. Her mother's warm hug was a comfort, her father's reassuring pat on the back a sign of his silent pride. Isabella's younger brother, who had grown a few inches taller since they last met, greeted her with a mix of excitement and curiosity.

Over the next few days, Isabella's home was a haven of joy. Her mother prepared all her favourite dishes—rich, spicy curries and fragrant biryanis that reminded her of her childhood. The laughter and chatter around the dinner table made Isabella realise how much she had missed these simple moments of togetherness. The family spent their evenings reminiscing about old times, sharing stories of their daily lives, and making plans for the future.

Sophia's reunion with her family was equally heartwarming. Her parents had decorated their home with bright flowers and balloons, making it feel like a celebration. Sophia's mother, always known for her impeccable cooking, had prepared a feast of delicacies that brought tears of joy to Sophia's eyes. Her father's jovial laughter and her younger sister's playful antics created an atmosphere of pure happiness.

The time spent at home allowed Sophia to reflect on the changes in her life. She and her family gathered in the living room, sharing their experiences and talking about their dreams and aspirations. They discussed Sophia's recent achievements and her plans for the future, her parents expressing their pride and admiration for her bravery and dedication.

Elena's visit was marked by a series of heartwarming reunions. Her family had been eagerly awaiting her return, and the emotional embrace from her parents was a testament to their love and support. They were glad to know that Elena's sister Erica is expecting a child. Elena had organised a small party in her honour. The celebration was filled with laughter, music, and heartfelt conversations, creating new memories to cherish.

Amelia's house was next, and her family was a stark contrast to the others. They laughed and joked, making the girls feel at ease, but even here, the anxiety was present. Amelia's younger brother, always the curious one, kept asking questions about their time in Dubai, about the strange, dangerous people they might have met. Amelia brushed it off, but her mind was racing. How could she explain the fear that still gripped them all?

Finally, they reached Olivia's house. The reunion with her family was the most emotional. Olivia's parents had been through a lot in the years they were away, and now, seeing their daughter back home, they couldn't stop the tears.

They sat together late into the night, talking about everything and nothing. But the conversation kept circling back to one thing: safety. Olivia's father, a former police officer, sensed something was wrong. He had been asking questions, piecing together the puzzle of their uneasy silence.

As the night drew to a close, the girls regrouped at their rented house. The city was quiet now, the chaos of the day replaced by the stillness of the night. They sat together in the living room, the weight of the day's reunions heavy on their shoulders.

"We have to do something," Isabella finally said, breaking the silence.

The others nodded in agreement. They had been running from the fear, trying to bury it in the excitement of starting college, of being back in Mumbai. But Queen Nickolav's threat was real, and it was time they faced it.

"We need to find out what she wants," Elena said, her voice steady despite the fear in her eyes.

"And we need to make sure our families are safe," Sophia added.

They all agreed. The days ahead would be challenging, but they were in this together. The bond they shared was stronger than any fear, and they knew that together, they could face whatever came their way.

As the first light of dawn crept into the room, the girls made a pact. They would protect each other and their families, no matter what. The shadows of Mumbai might be dark, but they were not afraid. Not anymore.

As they navigated the complexities of their new lives and old threats, the Sisterhood remained united, their bond forged in the fires of past adversities and their commitment to justice stronger than ever. Each step they took in Mumbai was a reminder of their past struggles and a step towards confronting the shadows that continued to haunt them.

Chapter 2
Echoes of the Past

The early morning light streamed through the curtains, casting long shadows across the room where the five friends sat huddled together. The night's conversation had left them with an uneasy resolve. As much as they wanted to enjoy their return to Mumbai, the memories of Queen Nickolav's threat loomed over them like a dark cloud.

Isabella broke the silence first, her voice barely above a whisper. "What do we actually know about her?"

Elena, who had been staring out the window, turned to face the group. "Not much. Just that she's dangerous and that she runs a trafficking ring. But the question is—why us?"

Sophia shuddered at the thought. "We didn't do anything… did we?" Her mind flashed back to the wedding, to the moment she had answered that call. The voice on the other end, dripping with malice, had sent chills down her spine then, and the memory of it still made her heart race.

Amelia frowned. "Maybe it's not about what we did, but about what we know. There has to be something that ties us to her."

"Or someone," Olivia added, her eyes narrowing in thought. "Maybe it's someone we've met, someone who has a connection to her. It can't be a coincidence that she targeted us."

Elena's phone buzzed, interrupting the conversation. She glanced at the screen—another unknown number. Her heart skipped a beat as she hesitated, then decided to answer.

"Hello?"

There was a brief silence on the other end, followed by the same cold, familiar voice. "You're running out of time, girls. Leave this alone, or the flames will consume you."

Elena's breath caught in her throat. "What do you want from us?"

A low chuckle echoed through the line. "I want you to remember that there are consequences for meddling in things you don't understand. This is your final warning."

The call disconnected, leaving Elena staring at her phone in stunned silence.

"What did she say?" Olivia asked, her voice trembling slightly.

Elena repeated the words, her voice shaking. "She said we're running out of time… and that this is our final warning."

The room fell silent, each of them processing the implications. The threat wasn't just a distant memory; it was real, and it was happening now.

"We need to figure this out," Amelia said firmly. "If she's warning us, then we're close to something. But what?"

Sophia's mind was racing, trying to piece together the fragments of their past that might hold the answers. "What if it has something to do with the wedding? That's when everything started."

Isabella nodded in agreement. "It's the only thing that makes sense. But what happened there that we don't remember?"

The girls fell into a deep silence, each trying to recall the events of that day. They had been so caught up in the joy of the wedding, the celebrations, and the excitement of being back in India, that they hadn't paid attention to anything else. But now, as they retraced their steps, small details began to emerge— things they had overlooked at the time.

"There was that man," Elena said suddenly, her voice filled with realisation. "The one who kept watching us from a distance. Do you remember?"

Amelia frowned. "I think so. He was at the wedding, right? I thought he was just one of the guests."

"But he wasn't," Olivia said, the pieces starting to fall into place. "I saw him outside the venue too, talking to someone. I didn't think much of it at the time, but now…"

"Now it makes sense," Sophia finished. "What if he's connected to Queen Nickolav? What if he was watching us for her?"

A cold shiver ran through the group as they realised they might have been under surveillance all along.

"We need to find out who he is," Isabella said, determination setting in. "And why was he there?".

"But how?" Elena asked. "We don't have much to go on."

"We start by asking questions," Olivia suggested. "We can talk to the wedding planner, check the guest list, see if anyone remembers him."

Amelia nodded. "And we can ask around the neighbourhood, see if anyone saw anything unusual that day."

The plan was set. They would start their investigation by

retracing their steps from the wedding, hoping to uncover the truth about the mysterious man and his connection to Queen Nickolav. It was a risky move, but they knew they had no other choice. If they wanted to protect themselves and their families, they needed to get to the bottom of this—no matter the cost.

As the sun climbed higher in the sky, the girls left Elena's house, each one filled with a mix of fear and determination. They had survived one threat, but they knew this was just the beginning. The echoes of the past were growing louder, and they had to be ready for whatever came next.

Little did they know, they were about to uncover secrets that would change their lives forever.

Chapter 3
Whispers in the Dark

The monsoon rains pounded against the windows of Elena's house, a relentless symphony of water and wind. The city of Mumbai was shrouded in a misty haze, the streets slick with rain. Inside, the girls huddled together, the weight of the previous night's conversation still heavy in the air. They had agreed to confront their fears, but the path ahead was unclear.

"We need a plan," Amelia said, breaking the silence that had settled over them. Her voice was determined, but her hands trembled slightly as she clutched her teacup.

Elena nodded, her mind racing. "I think we should start by finding out more about Queen Nickolav. We know she's dangerous, but we don't know much beyond that."

Olivia, who had been scrolling through her phone, looked up. "I've been researching her online, but there's not much. Most of what I found is just rumours—stories about her involvement in human trafficking, illegal arms deals, and other criminal activities. But there's nothing concrete."

Sophia leaned forward, her eyes intense. "What about the people in Dubai? We know she's based there. Maybe we could reach out to someone who might have information."

Isabella hesitated, her mind drifting back to their time in

Dubai. "I know a guy—Rami. He's well-connected in the underground scene there. If anyone knows about Nickolav, it's him. But I don't know if we can trust him."

The room fell silent again, the girls lost in thought. The rain outside seemed to grow louder, the sound of it almost deafening.

"We don't have a choice," Elena finally said, her voice quiet but resolute. "We have to take the risk. If Rami can give us information, it's worth it."

Olivia nodded in agreement. "Let's reach out to him. But we have to be careful. If Nickolav finds out we're looking into her, we could be in even more danger."

With their plan set, the girls prepared to contact Rami. Isabella pulled out her phone and composed a message, her fingers trembling slightly as she typed. "I'll ask him to meet us somewhere public," she said. "We'll be safer that way."

She hit send, and the message was out in the world, a small but significant step in their journey to uncover the truth. Now all they could do was wait.

The hours passed slowly, the tension in the room palpable. Finally, Isabella's phone buzzed. She picked it up, her heart racing. It was a reply from Rami: "Meet me at Café Arabica tomorrow at 3 PM. Come alone."

The girls exchanged worried glances. "He wants us to come alone," Isabella said, her voice barely above a whisper.

"No way," Amelia said firmly. "We're not splitting up. We'll all go, and we'll keep our distance. If anything happens, we can back each other up."

The next day, the girls arrived at Café Arabica, a small, inconspicuous coffee shop tucked away in a quiet corner of the city. The rain had finally stopped, leaving the streets damp and glistening under the afternoon sun. They took a table near the back, their eyes scanning the room for any sign of Rami.

He arrived a few minutes later, a tall, lean figure dressed in black, his face partially obscured by a hood. He walked over to their table, his movements smooth and deliberate.

"Isabella," he said, his voice low and smooth. "Long time no see."

"Rami," Isabella replied, trying to keep her voice steady. "Thanks for meeting us."

Rami sat down, his gaze flicking over the girls. "So, what do you need from me?"

Isabella hesitated for a moment before speaking. "We need information about Queen Nickolav. We know she's dangerous, and we've had some encounters with her. We need to know what we're dealing with."

Rami leaned back in his chair, a small smile playing on his lips. "Nickolav, huh? You're playing with fire, girls. But I guess you already know that."

He paused, his expression turning serious. "Nickolav is more than just a criminal. She's got connections everywhere—police, politicians, even some people in the media. She's untouchable. But she's also ruthless. If she sees you as a threat, she won't hesitate to eliminate you."

Sophia shivered at his words, her mind flashing back to the threatening call they had received. "What does she want with us? Why did she target us?"

Rami shrugged. "Could be a lot of things. Maybe you stumbled onto something you shouldn't have. Maybe someone close to you is involved with her. Or maybe she just enjoys the thrill of the chase. With Nickolav, you can never be sure."

Olivia spoke up, her voice trembling slightly. "Is there any way to stop her? To make her back off?"

Rami looked at her, his eyes dark. "There's only one way to stop someone like Nickolav. And trust me, you don't want to go down that road."

The girls exchanged uneasy glances. The stakes were higher than they had imagined, and the path ahead was fraught with danger.

"Is there anything else we should know?" Elena asked, her voice steady despite the fear gnawing at her.

Rami hesitated, then leaned in closer. "There's one thing. A rumour, really. They say Nickolav has a weakness—something from her past that she's desperate to keep hidden. If you can find out what it is, you might have a chance. But finding it won't be easy. And if she catches wind of what you're doing…"

He trailed off, the unspoken threat hanging in the air.

The girls sat in silence, the weight of Rami's words pressing down on them. They had come seeking answers, but all they had found were more questions—and a chilling realisation that their lives were in greater danger than ever before.

As Rami stood to leave, he gave them one last piece of advice. "Be careful, girls. In this game, one wrong move could be your last."

With that, he turned and walked out of the café, disappearing into the crowded streets of Mumbai.

The girls sat in silence for a long moment, absorbing everything they had just heard. They knew the road ahead would be treacherous, but they were determined to see it through. They had no choice.

"We'll find her weakness," Elena finally said, her voice filled with quiet resolve. "And when we do, we'll end this."

The others nodded, their fear giving way to a fierce determination. They were in this together, and they would face whatever came their way as a united front.

As they left the café and stepped back into the bustling streets of Mumbai, the sun had begun to set, casting long shadows over the city. But for the first time since their return, the girls felt a glimmer of hope.

They had a lead, a possible way to protect themselves and their families. And no matter how dark the path ahead, they were ready to face it.

Chapter 4
The Web Tightens

The narrow alleyways of Mumbai were labyrinthine, twisting and turning in ways that made them feel more like a maze than streets. As dusk settled over the city, the girls found themselves in one of these winding paths, the distant sounds of the bustling city barely reaching them. They were deep in the heart of Mumbai, far from the familiar comforts of home, following a lead that could bring them one step closer to understanding the enigma of Queen Nickolav.

Amelia had received a tip from a friend at college—a whispered conversation overheard in a dark corner of a library. It wasn't much, but it was something, a thread in the tangled web they were trying to unravel. The lead had pointed them to a small, unmarked building in this very alley, a place where the underworld of Mumbai might intersect with the remnants of Nickolav's shadowy empire.

"Are you sure this is the place?" Sophia asked, her voice tinged with doubt as they stood in front of the worn-out door, its paint peeling and the wood creaking ominously.

"This is where the tip led us," Amelia replied, though she didn't sound entirely convinced herself. "If there's any chance of finding information here, we have to take it."

Olivia, always the cautious one, looked around, her eyes scanning for any sign of danger. "We need to be careful. If this place is connected to Nickolav, we could be walking straight into a trap."

Elena stepped forward, her hand resting on the doorknob. "We've come this far. We can't turn back now."

With a deep breath, she pushed the door open. It creaked loudly, as if protesting their intrusion, but it gave way, revealing a dimly lit room that smelled of damp and decay. The girls exchanged nervous glances before stepping inside.

The room was sparse, with only a few pieces of broken furniture and a dusty counter that might have once served as a reception desk. Papers were scattered across the floor, some old and yellowed with age, others newer but still covered in a fine layer of dust. It was clear that this place had been abandoned for some time.

"This doesn't look promising," Isabella muttered, kicking a pile of papers aside with her foot. "Maybe the lead was a dead end."

But as she spoke, Olivia's eyes caught something—a small, almost hidden door at the back of the room, partially concealed by a heavy curtain. "Wait," she said, her voice sharp with sudden interest. "What's that?"

The girls moved cautiously towards the door. Olivia reached out and pulled the curtain aside, revealing a metal door with a rusted lock. It looked out of place in the otherwise decrepit room, as if it had been installed long after the building had fallen into disuse.

"This has to be it," Elena whispered, her heart pounding in her chest. "This door doesn't belong here."

Isabella knelt down, examining the lock. "It's old, but not too difficult to break. We just need something to force it open."

Amelia quickly found a piece of broken metal from one of the nearby tables and handed it to Isabella. With a few deft movements, Isabella managed to pry the lock open, the metal clanging as it hit the floor.

The door swung open, revealing a dark, narrow staircase leading downward. The air that wafted up from below was cool and damp, carrying with it the scent of something old and forgotten.

"Do we go down?" Sophia asked, her voice trembling slightly.

"We have to," Elena replied, her resolve hardening. "This could be where we find the answers we've been looking for."

One by one, they descended the stairs, their footsteps echoing in the confined space. The further down they went, the colder the air became, and the more oppressive the atmosphere grew. At the bottom of the stairs, they found themselves in a small, underground room.

The room was unlike anything they had expected. It was filled with rows of filing cabinets, each one meticulously labelled and organised. A single, bare lightbulb hung from the ceiling, casting a harsh glow over the room. It looked like some kind of archive, a place where records were kept—perhaps records of the very secrets they were seeking.

"This is it," Olivia said, her voice filled with awe. "This must be where Nickolav kept her records."

The girls quickly began searching through the cabinets, pulling out files and scanning the contents. The papers were filled with names, dates, transactions—evidence of Nickolav's extensive operations. But it was overwhelming, the sheer volume of information making it difficult to know where to start.

"Look for anything that mentions her weakness," Elena instructed, flipping through a thick file. "Rami said there might be something in her past, something she's desperate to keep hidden."

As they continued their search, Isabella came across a file that caught her attention. It was marked with a single word: "Khrustal'nyy." She opened it carefully, her eyes widening as she scanned the contents.

"Guys, I think I found something," she said, her voice urgent.

The others gathered around as Isabella read aloud. "It's a report—an old one, from years ago. It mentions a place called Khrustal'nyy, in Russia. There's something about an incident there, something involving Nickolav. It's vague, but it sounds important."

"Khrustal'nyy," Sophia repeated, the name unfamiliar on her tongue. "What happened there?"

"I'm not sure," Isabella replied, frowning as she continued to read. "But whatever it was, it was serious. There's a mention of a cover-up, of people being silenced. And... wait, there's a reference to a person. Someone named Mikhail. It says he was a key witness, but he disappeared shortly after the incident."

"Mikhail could be the key," Olivia said, her mind racing. "If we can find him, maybe we can learn what happened in Khrustal'nyy and use it against Nickolav."

"But how do we find someone who's been missing for years?" Amelia asked, her voice tinged with concern.

"We start by digging into this," Elena said, holding up the

file. "There's got to be more here. We can cross-reference the names, look for connections. We'll figure it out."

Just as they were about to continue their search, they heard a noise from above—a creak of footsteps on the stairs. The girls froze, their hearts racing.

"Someone's here," Isabella whispered, her voice filled with fear.

They quickly extinguished the light and huddled together in the darkness, their breaths shallow and their minds racing. The footsteps grew louder, closer, until they stopped right at the top of the stairs.

The door creaked open, and a beam of light sliced through the darkness. A figure stood at the top of the stairs, silhouetted against the dim light from above. For a moment, the girls held their breath, terrified that they had been discovered.

But after a long, tense moment, the door creaked shut, and the footsteps retreated back up the stairs. The girls waited in silence, their hearts pounding, until they were certain the intruder had left.

"We need to get out of here," Elena whispered, her voice shaking. "Now."

They quickly gathered the files they had found and stuffed them into their bags. Then, as quietly as they could, they made their way back up the stairs and out of the building, slipping into the night without looking back.

As they emerged into the safety of the crowded streets, the adrenaline still coursing through their veins, they knew that the web was tightening around them. They had uncovered something important—something that could be the key to bringing down Queen Nickolav.

But they also knew that the danger was greater than ever. Someone was watching them, and it was only a matter of time before they would have to face the full wrath of the woman who had cast such a long shadow over their lives.

Chapter 5
Unveiling the Unknown

The next few days passed in a blur as the girls pored over the files they had retrieved from the hidden archive. Their small apartment in Mumbai had transformed into a makeshift war room, with papers strewn across every surface, maps pinned to the walls, and a constant buzz of conversation as they pieced together the fragments of information. The name "Khrustal'nyy" had become their focus, and the elusive Mikhail, the key to unlocking the secrets of Queen Nickolav's past, was their goal.

But as they delved deeper into the mystery, another figure began to emerge from the shadows—a man who seemed to be one step ahead of them at every turn. They had encountered signs of him before: files that seemed to have been disturbed, phone calls that ended abruptly, and a feeling that someone else was hunting the same truth.

It was Olivia who first brought up the possibility. "What if there's someone else out there, looking for the same thing we are?" she asked one evening, as they sat around the table, their eyes bleary from hours of reading.

"You mean like a rival?" Isabella said, her brow furrowing. "Someone who wants to get to Nickolav before we do?"

"Or someone on our side," Elena suggested, a glimmer of hope in her voice. "Someone who knows what we're up against and wants to help."

Amelia leaned back in her chair, considering the idea. "If that's true, we need to find them. If they're after Nickolav too, we could work together. It might be the only way to take her down."

The decision was made to track down this mystery person, to find out who they were and what their intentions might be. They started by following the clues they had already encountered—the disturbed files, the strange phone calls, the places where they had felt that presence before.

It wasn't long before they got their first real lead.

One evening, while scanning through security footage from a café where they had been discussing their plans, Amelia spotted him—a man sitting alone at a table near the back, watching them intently. He was dressed inconspicuously, with a hat pulled low over his face, but there was no mistaking the fact that he had been listening to their conversation.

"Pause it there," Elena said, leaning in closer to the screen. "Can you zoom in?"

Amelia did as instructed, enhancing the image until the man's face was more visible. He was in his late twenties, with dark hair and a serious expression. There was something familiar about him, though none of the girls could quite place it.

"Who is he?" Sophia wondered aloud. "And why was he watching us?"

"I don't know," Isabella said, her eyes narrowing. "But I intend to find out."

The next day, they returned to the café, hoping to find the

mystery man again. They took a table near the back, keeping their voices low as they discussed their plans. They didn't have to wait long before he appeared.

He entered the café just as they had seen in the footage, his eyes scanning the room before settling on their table. For a moment, he hesitated, as if deciding whether or not to approach. Then, with a determined expression, he walked over to them.

"Mind if I join you?" he asked, his voice calm but carrying an undercurrent of tension.

The girls exchanged quick glances, unsure of how to respond. Finally, Elena nodded. "Sure, have a seat."

He sat down, removing his hat and placing it on the table. Up close, he looked even more serious, his eyes dark and focused. There was a quiet intensity about him, as if he was carrying a heavy burden.

"I'm not here to hurt you," he began, sensing their unease. "In fact, I think we might have a common goal."

"You've been following us," Olivia said, her tone cautious but curious. "Why?"

"Because you're after the same thing I am," he replied, his gaze steady. "Queen Nickolav."

The girls tensed at the mention of her name, but they didn't speak, waiting for him to continue.

"My name is Alexei," he said, introducing himself. "I've been tracking Nickolav for years, ever since she destroyed my family. My parents... they were activists, journalists who tried to expose her crimes. She had them killed, making it look like an accident. But I know the truth. I've spent my life gathering evidence, trying to bring her down. But she's powerful, too powerful for one person to take on alone."

"Why didn't you approach us sooner?" Isabella asked, suspicion still lingering in her voice.

"I wasn't sure if I could trust you," Alexei admitted. "I've been betrayed before, by people who pretended to be on my side. But after seeing how determined you are, how close you've come to finding the truth... I realised we're stronger together."

Elena studied him carefully. There was a sincerity in his eyes, a deep-seated anger that mirrored their own. She believed him, though she wasn't entirely ready to let her guard down.

"We've found some information," she said cautiously. "About a place called Khrustal'nyy, and someone named Mikhail. Do you know anything about that?"

Alexei's expression darkened at the mention of Khrustal'nyy. "I've heard of it. It's a town in Russia, isolated, hidden away from the world. There was an incident there years ago, something Nickolav was involved in. Mikhail... if he's still alive, he could be the key to exposing her. But finding him won't be easy. Nickolav has a long reach, and she's been covering her tracks for years."

"Then we'll need your help," Sophia said, her voice steady. "If we're going to do this, we need to work together."

Alexei nodded, a sense of determination settling over him. "Agreed. But we need to move quickly. Nickolav's already aware that someone is after her. If she finds out we're working together, she'll stop at nothing to destroy us."

The girls exchanged glances, a silent agreement passing between them. They had found an ally in Alexei, someone who understood the danger they were facing and was just as committed to bringing Queen Nickolav down. But they also knew that their task had just become even more dangerous.

"Let's start by finding Mikhail," Alexei said, his voice resolute. "If we can locate him, we might finally have the leverage we need."

With their new ally by their side, the girls felt a renewed sense of purpose. They had uncovered the first real piece of the puzzle, but there were still many mysteries left to solve. The shadows were closing in around them, and the stakes were higher than ever. But together, they were stronger, and they were ready to face whatever came next.

As the group begins their search for Mikhail, they dive deeper into the dangerous underworld that Queen Nickolav controls. With Alexei's help, they uncover new leads and face new challenges, all while trying to stay one step ahead of Nickolav's forces. The alliance they've formed will be tested as they venture into the unknown, where every choice could be the difference between life and death.

Chapter 6
The Unmasking

The tension in the room was palpable as Alexei sat across from the girls, his expression grim. The revelation of Queen Nickolav's connection to the town of Khrustal'nyy had been a significant breakthrough, but Alexei had promised them more—something darker and more insidious. The atmosphere was heavy with anticipation as they waited for him to speak.

"You know Nickolav as a ruthless criminal, a trafficker, and a shadowy figure with her hands in countless illegal operations," Alexei began, his voice low and steady. "But what you don't know is that she's also behind a massive fraud scheme—one that's been preying on the most vulnerable in society: the elderly."

The girls leaned in closer, their interest piqued.

"Over the past few years," Alexei continued, "Nickolav has orchestrated a network of fake charitable trusts and bogus insurance schemes. On the surface, these operations appear legitimate, offering elderly people promises of security in their twilight years—retirement plans, health insurance, and donations to causes they care about. But in reality, it's all a front."

Elena frowned, her mind racing. "A front for what?"

"For syphoning off their life savings," Alexei replied, his eyes flashing with anger. "These trusts are nothing more than elaborate scams. They lure in the elderly with promises of peace of mind, but the money they hand over never goes to the charities or insurance policies they think they're supporting. Instead, it disappears into Nickolav's pockets, funding her criminal empire."

"Does that mean the people are left with nothing?" Isabella asked, horrified by the thought.

"Exactly," Alexei confirmed. "And when they try to access their so-called benefits or seek help from these trusts, they find that the organisations no longer exist. The phone numbers are disconnected, the offices are empty, and the people behind them have vanished. It's like they never existed."

"How does she manage to pull this off on such a large scale?" Amelia asked, trying to comprehend the enormity of the scheme.

"It's a combination of manipulation, fear, and exploitation," Alexei explained. "She uses trusted community figures—doctors, lawyers, even priests—to vouch for these schemes. People believe them because they trust the person recommending it. And by the time they realise something is wrong, it's too late."

Sophia clenched her fists, the injustice of it all making her blood boil. "And no one's done anything to stop her?"

"People have tried," Alexei said, his voice tinged with bitterness. "But she's smart. She uses shell companies, fake identities, and bribes to cover her tracks. Even when someone does manage to expose part of the operation, they're quickly silenced—either by legal threats, blackmail, or worse."

Olivia's eyes narrowed as she processed the information.

"This is more than just a scam—it's a betrayal of trust on a massive scale. These people are being robbed of their dignity and their security."

"That's exactly what it is," Alexei agreed. "And it's why I've been working so hard to bring her down. My parents were investigating a similar scheme when they were killed. They were close to uncovering the full extent of Nickolav's fraud, but she got to them before they could expose her."

The room fell silent as the weight of Alexei's words sank in. The girls had known they were up against a formidable foe, but the scope of Nickolav's cruelty was staggering.

"What can we do?" Elena asked finally, her voice filled with determination. "How can we stop this?"

"There's only one way," Alexei replied. "We need to find the proof. We need to expose her entire operation—names, dates, transactions, everything. If we can do that, we can bring her down for good. But it won't be easy. She's covered her tracks well, and she won't go down without a fight."

"We're ready," Olivia said firmly, speaking for all of them. "Whatever it takes, we're going to see this through."

Alexei nodded, a flicker of respect in his eyes. "Then we'll start with the files you found in the archive. There might be clues in there—connections between her various operations that we can trace back to the trusts and insurance frauds. We'll need to cross-reference everything, find the patterns, and identify the key players."

"Let's get to work," Isabella said, her voice resolute.

The next few hours were a blur of activity. The girls and Alexei worked together, sifting through the files, tracing leads, and mapping out the connections between Nickolav's various schemes. It was painstaking work, but with each piece of the puzzle they uncovered, the picture became clearer.

They discovered that the fraudulent trusts were often linked to legitimate charities, using their names to gain credibility. In some cases, Nickolav's operatives had even infiltrated these charities, using their positions to divert funds and manipulate records. The insurance scams were similarly sophisticated, with policies that appeared real but were completely fabricated, leaving the victims with worthless documents.

As they pieced together the evidence, they began to see a pattern—certain names kept appearing in the documents, individuals who seemed to be at the center of the operations. One name in particular stood out: Viktor Ivanov, a man who appeared to be the linchpin in Nickolav's financial network.

"This Viktor Ivanov," Elena said, pointing to the name on the map they had created, "he's connected to almost every one of these schemes. If we can find him, we might be able to unravel the entire operation."

"He's the key," Alexei agreed. "But finding him won't be easy. He's a ghost, just like Nickolav. He uses aliases, moves around constantly, and keeps a low profile. But he's also greedy, and that might be his weakness."

"What do you mean?" Sophia asked.

"If we can lure him out with the promise of a big score," Alexei explained, "we might be able to trap him. We could set up a fake trust, something so lucrative that he can't resist getting involved. Once he takes the bait, we can expose him."

"But we'll need to be careful," Olivia cautioned. "If he suspects anything, he'll disappear, and we'll lose our chance."

"We'll need to plan this carefully," Amelia said, her mind

already racing with possibilities. "We need to make it look real, convincing enough that he won't suspect a thing."

The plan was risky, and the stakes were high, but it was their best chance at taking down Nickolav's operation. The girls knew that if they succeeded, they could save countless others from falling victim to the same cruel scam.

As they finalised their plans, the sense of urgency grew. Time was running out, and Nickolav was likely already aware that someone was getting close to exposing her. But with Alexei's help, they were determined to see this through to the end.

Chapter 7:
Shadows of Khrustal'nyy

The air inside the dimly lit room felt heavy with anticipation as the girls and Alexei stared at the map in front of them, tracing the route to the remote Russian town of Khrustal'nyy. The town had emerged as a pivotal piece in their puzzle, a place shrouded in mystery, tied to Queen Nickolav's dark past. Somewhere within its borders, Mikhail, the man who could bring down Nickolav, was hiding—or so they hoped.

"Khrustal'nyy isn't just a place," Alexei began, his voice low. "It's a graveyard of secrets. The town was abandoned years ago, but for a brief period, it was a hub of illegal operations—trafficking, corruption, and unspeakable horrors. Nickolav built her empire from the ruins of that town."

"Why there?" Isabella asked, studying the map. "What's so special about Khrustal'nyy?"

Alexei leaned back in his chair, his gaze dark. "Because it's hidden. Isolated. No one goes there anymore, and those who do either don't come back or are never the same again. The locals used to call it the town of ghosts. But the real secret lies in the people who vanished there—people who knew too much about Nickolav's operations."

Elena, who had been quiet, finally spoke. "And Mikhail?

He's connected to Khrustal'nyy?"

"Yes," Alexei said, nodding. "Mikhail was once one of Nickolav's closest allies, a man who knew everything about her rise to power. But he turned on her after witnessing the horrors she orchestrated in that town. He disappeared not long after, and the last trace of him leads back to Khrustal'nyy. If he's still alive, he's hiding there."

The room fell silent as the gravity of the situation sank in. Khrustal'nyy wasn't just another step in their journey—it was a descent into a forgotten place, one where Nickolav's influence still lingered like a dark cloud.

"We have no choice, then," Olivia said, breaking the silence. "If Mikhail is there, we need to find him. He's the only one who can help us expose Nickolav."

"But it's not just about finding him," Alexei warned. "Khrustal'nyy is dangerous. Nickolav still has people there— loyalists who will do anything to protect her secrets. They'll be watching for anyone who gets too close."

"I'm not afraid," Amelia said firmly. "We've come this far. We can't turn back now."

Alexei studied the girls, his expression unreadable. Finally, he nodded. "Then we'll go together. But we need to be prepared. Once we set foot in Khrustal'nyy, there's no turning back."

A week later, the group found themselves standing at the edge of the desolate town. The journey had been long and perilous, taking them deep into the Russian wilderness. The roads leading to Khrustal'nyy were nearly impassable, overgrown with vegetation and crumbling from years of neglect. The sky above was a grey, casting a spell over the landscape.

"This place gives me the creeps," Sophia muttered, pulling

her jacket tighter around herself as a cold wind swept through the barren streets.

Isabella nodded, her eyes scanning the empty buildings that lined the road. "It feels like time forgot this place."

The town itself was a ghost of what it once was. Dilapidated houses stood in eerie silence, their windows shattered and doors hanging off their hinges. Overgrown vines crawled up the walls, reclaiming the ruins. An unsettling silence blanketed Khrustal'nyy, broken only by the distant rustling of leaves and the occasional creak of a collapsing structure.

"Stay close," Alexei instructed, his voice barely above a whisper. "We need to find Mikhail before they find us."

As they ventured deeper into the town, the oppressive atmosphere grew more intense. Every shadow seemed to move, and every sound felt like an impending threat. The narrow streets twisted and turned, leading them deeper into the heart of Khrustal'nyy.

They finally reached a crumbling building at the far end of town—an old schoolhouse, its roof caved in and walls covered in graffiti. According to Alexei, this was the last known location of Mikhail. It was here, among the forgotten ruins of Khrustal'nyy, that they would find their answers.

"I don't like this," Olivia whispered as they approached the building. "It feels like a trap."

"It might be," Alexei admitted. "But we don't have a choice."

Carefully, they stepped inside the decrepit building, their footsteps echoing in the vast emptiness. The air was thick with dust, and the smell of decay was overwhelming. Broken desks and chairs littered the floor, remnants of a place once filled with life, now reduced to ruin.

"We need to split up," Alexei said quietly. "Search for any signs that Mikhail's been here. But stay alert. If you see anything suspicious, call out."

The girls nodded and fanned out, their senses on high alert as they moved through the abandoned school. The silence was unnerving, and every creak of the floorboards felt like a warning.

Elena was the first to find something. In a small, dimly lit room at the back of the building, she discovered a stack of old notebooks and papers. Most of it was illegible, damaged by years of neglect, but one document caught her eye—a map of Khrustal'nyy with certain locations circled in red.

"Guys," she called out, her voice echoing through the empty halls. "I found something."

The others quickly joined her, gathering around the map. Alexei's eyes widened as he studied it.

"This... this is Mikhail's handwriting," he said, his voice tense. "These marked locations—they're safe houses. Places he might have hidden when he was on the run."

"So he was here," Isabella said, her voice filled with both relief and fear. "He might still be."

"We need to check these locations," Alexei said, his voice urgent. "But we need to be careful. If Mikhail was using these places, Nickolav's people might have found them too."

With the map as their guide, they set off to explore the marked locations. The first two safe houses were abandoned, showing no signs of life, but at the third, they found something. The door was barricaded from the inside, and faint footsteps could be heard coming from within.

Alexei knocked on the door, his voice firm but calm. "Mikhail? It's me, Alexei. We need to talk."

For a moment, there was only silence. Then, the sound of locks being undone echoed through the building. The door creaked open, revealing a haggard man with unkempt hair and a gaunt face. His eyes were filled with fear and suspicion, but there was also a flicker of recognition as he looked at Alexei.

"Mikhail," Alexei said, relief flooding his voice. "You're alive."

Mikhail nodded slowly, his gaze shifting to the girls. "Who are they?" he asked, his voice hoarse from disuse.

"They're on our side," Alexei assured him. "We're here to take down Nickolav. We need your help."

Mikhail hesitated for a moment, then stepped aside, allowing them into the safe house. Inside, the room was sparse, with only a few scattered belongings and a makeshift bed. It was clear that Mikhail had been living in fear, constantly on the run.

"You don't know what you're up against," Mikhail said, his voice trembling slightly. "Nickolav... she's not just a criminal. She's a monster. She's destroyed everything in her path, and she'll destroy you too if you're not careful."

"We know the risks," Elena said, her voice steady. "But we're not turning back now. We need to expose her—everything she's done, including what happened here in Khrustal'nyy."

Mikhail looked at them, his eyes filled with both fear and admiration. "Then you're braver than I ever was. I'll help you. But you need to be prepared for what you'll find."

As they sat down to talk, the shadows of Khrustal'nyy seemed to close in around them. The town held more secrets than they could have imagined, and Mikhail was about to reveal the darkest of them all.

Chapter 8
Secrets of the Past

The dim light inside the safe house flickered as Mikhail sat down with the girls and Alexei, his hands trembling slightly. He took a deep breath, the weight of years of fear and silence pressing down on him. Outside, the ghost town of Khrustal'nyy remained eerily quiet, but inside this room, the past was about to come to life—Nickolav's past.

"You think you know her," Mikhail began, his voice raspy and full of emotion. "But what you've seen is only the tip of the iceberg. Nickolav wasn't always a criminal mastermind. She wasn't always a monster."

The girls exchanged glances, unsure of what to expect next. They had faced ruthless opponents before, but something in Mikhail's tone hinted at a darker, more personal story.

"Her real name is Veronika Ivanovna Rykova," Mikhail continued. "She was born in Khrustal'nyy—long before it became what it is now. This town, once bustling with life, was where her story began. She was the daughter of a well-known Soviet general and a local school teacher. But her childhood wasn't what it seemed."

Elena leaned in; her interest piqued. "What happened?"

"Her father was a man of power, but also cruel," Mikhail

said, his voice lowering. "He ruled this town with an iron fist, enforcing Soviet doctrines without mercy. Those who disobeyed or questioned the system disappeared—sent to labour camps or worse. Veronika grew up watching her father destroy lives, and as she got older, she began to emulate him. But she wasn't satisfied with just enforcing her father's rules. She wanted more."

Sophia frowned. "So, she became like him?"

Mikhail shook his head. "No. She became worse. Her father's methods were brutal, but predictable. Veronika... she thrived on chaos, manipulating people, making them believe she was their saviour while pulling the strings behind their backs. She started small—running underground schemes right here in Khrustal'nyy, convincing people she could help them escape her father's wrath. She built trust, earned loyalty, but all of it was a lie."

Amelia's eyes widened in shock. "She was scamming them even back then?"

"Yes," Mikhail replied, nodding gravely. "She betrayed everyone who trusted her. Her father found out, but instead of punishing her, he saw potential. He took her under his wing and taught her the art of control, how to use fear to manipulate people. But Veronika had bigger ambitions. She didn't want to be confined to Khrustal'nyy—she wanted to rule beyond these borders."

"And that's when she became Nickolav?" Olivia asked.

Mikhail hesitated, then nodded. "Yes. After her father died, Veronika took on the name 'Nickolav' and began her rise to power. She used the connections her father had built in the Soviet regime and expanded them. First, it was arms dealing, then drug trafficking, and eventually, human trafficking. But she didn't stop there. The charitable trust scam you uncovered was just one of many ways she made her empire impenetrable. She diversified, using her criminal operations to fund 'legitimate' businesses. That's why she's so hard to bring down. She has layers of protection."

Isabella's voice wavered with disgust. "And Khrustal'nyy... what did she do to this town?"

Mikhail's face darkened. "This town is the cornerstone of her empire. After the Soviet Union collapsed, she returned here to use it as a base. No one noticed what was happening because Khrustal'nyy was already fading into obscurity. She took advantage of the chaos and transformed the town into her own personal kingdom. People who came here seeking refuge or escape ended up trapped, forced into labour or sold into trafficking rings. The town became a factory for her operations."

Elena's heart sank as the full scope of Nickolav's evil came into focus. "And the people? The ones who lived here?"

"Most of them are gone," Mikhail said quietly. "Those who resisted vanished. The others... they worked for her or became victims themselves. Some even became part of her inner circle, fearing for their own lives. She has a way of making people believe they have no choice."

Alexei's jaw tightened; the anger evident on his face. "She's not invincible. We know her secrets now. If we can expose her past—everything she did here—we can bring her down."

"But it's not that simple," Mikhail warned. "Nickolav is always a step ahead. She has eyes everywhere, even here in Khrustal'nyy. She's been hiding her past for years, burying anyone who tries to dig it up. If she knows we're here, she won't hesitate to kill us all."

"We can't stop now," Elena said firmly. "We need to show the world who she really is."

"We have to be smart about it," Alexei added. "We can't just rely on Mikhail's testimony. We need physical evidence— proof that ties Nickolav to everything that happened in Khrustal'nyy."

Mikhail stood up slowly and walked to a small, dusty chest in the corner of the room. He opened it and pulled out a thick stack of documents, yellowed with age. "I've been collecting evidence for years. I couldn't leave this town without trying to right the wrongs I witnessed. Everything I've gathered is here— names, transactions, contracts, even personal letters. But it's dangerous. These documents are Nickolav's greatest fear, and if she knows we have them..."

"We'll make sure they get out," Olivia assured him. "This is our chance to expose her once and for all."

As they gathered around the stack of documents, the weight of what they were about to undertake hit them. Queen Nickolav's past was filled with horrors they could barely comprehend, and her present was even more dangerous. But now, they had the means to take her down.

"We need to move quickly," Alexei said, urgency in his voice. "If we stay here too long, she'll come after us."

Mikhail nodded; his eyes haunted. "I'll help you. But once we leave Khrustal'nyy, there's no going back. We'll be targets, and Nickolav won't stop until we're all dead."

"We know the risks," Elena said, standing tall. "But we're not afraid."

As they prepared to leave Khrustal'nyy, carrying the weight

of Nickolav's dark past with them, the group realised they were stepping into the final phase of their mission. The secrets of the past had been unearthed, and now it was time to expose them to the world.

But in the shadows, Nickolav's loyalists were already closing in, and the battle to bring down the Queen was just beginning.

Chapter 9:
The Escape from Khrustal'nyy

The frigid Russian night bit at their skin as the group hurriedly made their way out of Khrustal'nyy. The wind howled, carrying an eerie reminder of the town's desolate state. Elena, Isabella, Sophia, Amelia, Olivia, Alexei, and Mikhail moved silently, careful to avoid drawing attention. Every shadow seemed like a potential threat; every sound made their hearts race.

They had just reached the outskirts of the town, their bags filled with documents that could take down Queen Nickolav. These papers were the key to revealing the full extent of her crimes. But they knew the hardest part was still ahead—getting out alive.

Alexei led the group, his eyes scanning the perimeter, his hand tightly gripping his gun. "We need to get to the car, fast. We can't afford to be seen."

Behind him, Mikhail walked with the weight of years of secrecy pressing on his shoulders. He had been hiding for so long, and now that they were close to exposing the truth, fear gnawed at him. "If they catch us before we make it out of here..."

"They won't," Olivia said, her voice steady. "We've come too far to lose now."

Sophia, on the other hand, couldn't shake the unease that had been building inside her since they left the safe house. "Something doesn't feel right. It's too quiet."

Just as the words left her mouth, a loud crack echoed through the night. They all froze, tension coiling in the air like a viper ready to strike.

"Get down!" Alexei barked, pulling his gun as the group dropped to the ground, scrambling for cover behind the nearest building. The echo of footsteps filled the air. The enemy had arrived.

"They found us," Mikhail whispered, his face pale.

From the darkened streets of Khrustal'nyy, figures emerged—Nickolav's loyalists. They were well-trained and heavily armed, moving with precision and intent. Elena's heart pounded in her chest as she peered around the corner. There was at least a dozen of them, closing in fast.

"We're surrounded," Isabella said, her voice barely above a whisper. "How do we get out of here?"

Alexei's face was grim. "We'll have to fight our way through. They know what we have—they won't let us leave alive."

Elena's mind raced, her thoughts flickering between fear and resolve. "We have to protect the documents at all costs."

"There's an abandoned building just ahead," Alexei pointed out. "We need to make it there and barricade ourselves. It'll buy us time to come up with a plan."

Amelia nodded, already gripping the handle of the bag that held the precious documents. "Let's move."

They sprinted toward the building, bullets whizzing past them as Nickolav's men opened fire. The sound of gunshots shattered the quiet night, but adrenaline pushed the group forward. They darted between crumbling structures and dodged the hail of bullets, hearts racing as they neared the safety of the building.

Amelia reached the door first, slamming it open. One by one, they rushed inside. Alexei, the last to enter, fired off a few shots to cover their retreat before shutting the door behind them. They quickly barricaded it with anything they could find—old furniture, broken chairs, and debris.

Sophia leaned against the wall, catching her breath. "How long do you think we have?"

"Not long," Alexei said, his tone grim. "They'll break through eventually."

"Is there another way out?" Olivia asked, scanning the room for exits.

"There's a back door," Mikhail said, pointing to a rusted metal door at the rear of the room. "But it leads to a narrow alley. If they find us, we'll be trapped."

Elena paced back and forth, her mind racing for a solution. They couldn't stay here forever. The longer they waited, the closer Nickolav's men would get. They had to act fast.

"Is there any way to contact help?" Isabella asked, her voice strained with urgency.

"We've been cut off since we entered Khrustal'nyy," Alexei replied, shaking his head. "Nickolav has the town wired. The only way to call for help is to get outside her perimeter."

"What if we create a distraction?" Amelia suggested, her eyes bright with an idea. "We can lead them away from the documents. They're after the evidence, right? If they think we still have it, they'll follow us."

Olivia nodded, catching on. "We split up. One group takes

the documents, the other creates a diversion.”

“It’s risky,” Alexei said, weighing the options. “But it might be our only chance.”

“We don’t have time to argue,” Elena said firmly. “Amelia, Olivia, and I will take the documents. Alexei, you, Sophia, and Isabella distract them.”

Alexei frowned. “Are you sure you can handle it?”

Elena’s eyes were fierce with determination. “We’ve come this far. We’re not backing down now.”

The plan was quickly set in motion. Alexei, Sophia, and Isabella would stay behind, setting off a series of makeshift traps and diversions to draw Nickolav’s men away from the back exit. Meanwhile, Elena, Amelia, and Olivia would make a run for it with the documents.

As they prepared to leave, Mikhail approached Elena. “You’re doing the right thing. But be careful—Nickolav won’t rest until she has those documents.”

Elena nodded, gripping the bag tightly. “We won’t let her win.”

With a final glance at the others, Elena led Amelia and Olivia through the back door, slipping into the narrow alley. The cold air hit them again, but they pushed forward, moving as quickly and quietly as they could. Behind them, they heard the first of Alexei’s distractions—a loud crash followed by shouting.

“They’re going for it,” Amelia whispered, her eyes darting around. “Let’s move.”

The three of them navigated through the dark alleys of Khrustal’nyy, careful to stay in the shadows. They could still hear the sounds of fighting from the main street, but with any luck, Alexei’s plan would buy them enough time to escape.

Just as they neared the edge of town, a sharp voice cut through the air. "Stop right there!"

Elena's heart dropped. Standing in front of them was a tall, muscular man, his gun raised and pointed directly at them. Behind him, two more of Nickolav's men appeared, blocking their path.

"We've got you now," the man sneered. "Hand over the documents, and maybe we'll let you live."

Olivia's eyes flashed with anger. "You don't scare us."

The man's smile widened. "You should be scared, little girl. You have no idea who you're dealing with."

Elena tightened her grip on the bag, her mind racing. They were outnumbered, and there was no clear way out. But they couldn't let Nickolav's men get the documents.

Amelia glanced at Elena, her voice barely a whisper. "What do we do?"

Elena's heart pounded in her chest, but her gaze remained steady. They had come too far to fail now. With a deep breath, she made her decision.

"We fight."

The confrontation that followed was fast and brutal. The girls moved with precision and determination, using their environment to their advantage. Olivia knocked one of the men off balances with a swift kick, while Amelia disarmed the second with a well-placed punch. Elena, meanwhile, faced off with the leader, her eyes burning with resolve.

"You're making a big mistake," he growled, swinging his gun at her.

Elena dodged the blow, grabbing a nearby metal pipe and countering his attack. "No, the mistake was thinking we wouldn't fight back."

In the end, it was Olivia who delivered the final blow, knocking the leader unconscious with a swift strike. Panting, the girls stood over the fallen men, their hearts racing with adrenaline.

"We need to go," Amelia urged, picking up the bag. "They'll send more."

Elena nodded, her eyes hard with determination. "We can't stop now. Let's finish this."

As they left the town of Khrustal'nyy behind, the weight of what they had just survived began to settle in. The documents were still safe, but they knew the fight was far from over. Nickolav's reach extended far beyond the borders of this ghost town, and the real battle was just beginning.

But for now, they had won a small victory. And with the secrets of Khrustal'nyy in their hands, they were one step closer to bringing down the queen.

Chapter 10:
The Betrayal Within

The safe house in Moscow was dimly lit, its walls lined with dusty shelves and old furniture, providing the perfect cover for their operations. Elena, Amelia, Olivia, Isabella, and Sophia had gathered around a table cluttered with documents and laptops, while Alexei stood by the window, scanning the streets below for any signs of trouble. Outside, the city was alive with the noise of traffic and distant sirens, but inside, the tension was palpable.

"We need to get this out before it's too late," Elena said, her voice tight with urgency. "Nickolav's empire can't survive once this information is made public. These documents show everything—how she's defrauding elderly people, running her human trafficking operations, and laundering money through the fake charitable trusts."

Amelia nodded as she tapped away at her laptop. "I'm preparing encrypted copies of the files to send to trusted journalists and law enforcement. Once they go live, there's no going back."

"But we need to be careful," Olivia added. "If Nickolav finds out what we're doing before we're ready, she'll retaliate. And hard."

Sophia, sitting quietly in the corner, seemed lost in thought. Her mind had been racing ever since their escape from Khrustal'nyy. Something was gnawing at her, a feeling she couldn't shake. "I don't know why, but I have this bad feeling," she admitted, her voice soft but uneasy. "Like we're missing something."

Isabella looked up from her notes. "We've covered every angle, every escape route. But you're right—we should be on high alert."

Suddenly, Alexei turned away from the window, his brow furrowed in concern. "We might have a bigger problem. I just saw a black SUV circling the block. It's the second time in ten minutes."

Elena's heart skipped a beat. "You think it's Nickolav's men?"

"I wouldn't be surprised," Alexei said grimly. "They've been tracking us since we left Khrustal'nyy. We bought ourselves some time, but it looks like she's closing in."

Amelia's fingers flew across the keyboard, her anxiety rising. "We need to move faster. The files are almost ready to send, but we're going to need a new location soon. If they're watching us, we're not safe here."

Just as the tension in the room began to spike, Mikhail entered the room, his expression unreadable. He had been keeping a low profile ever since they'd arrived in Moscow, avoiding contact with anyone outside the group. But now, something about his demeanor seemed different—cold, distant.

"We need to talk," Mikhail said, his eyes locking with Alexei's. "Privately."

Alexei frowned, but nodded, following Mikhail into the next

room.

Inside the small, cramped space, Mikhail closed the door and turned to Alexei. His eyes were hard, calculating.

"We've made it this far, but there's something I need you to understand," Mikhail said, his voice low. "Nickolav... She's not just any criminal. She's built her empire on secrets, alliances, and leverage. And right now, we're walking straight into her trap."

"What are you talking about?" Alexei asked, his face darkening.

Mikhail sighed, running a hand through his greying hair. "Nickolav already knows what we're doing. She's been ahead of us this entire time. She's just waiting for us to make a mistake."

Alexei's jaw clenched. "How could she know? We've been careful."

"Because she has someone on the inside," Mikhail said, his words heavy with meaning. "Someone close to you."

The realisation hit Alexei like a punch to the gut. His mind raced through the possibilities. Could it be one of the girls? Someone in their group had betrayed them?

"Who?" Alexei demanded, his voice a low growl.

Mikhail hesitated, his gaze faltering for the first time. "Sophia."

Alexei's blood ran cold. "That's impossible. Sophia's been with us since the beginning. She would never betray us."

"Are you sure about that?" Mikhail countered. "Nickolav has ways of turning people, using their fears and weaknesses against them. She's ruthless. And Sophia... she's been acting strange, hasn't she? Distant, quiet. Something changed after the wedding incident in India, after that threatening call from Nickolav. I think Nickolav got to her back then."

Alexei's mind raced. He thought back to Sophia's behaviour—her quietness, her hesitation. But could she really be working with Nickolav? It seemed unthinkable.

Before he could respond, there was a loud crash from the other room.

Elena and the others had been working diligently when the sound of breaking glass shattered their focus. They jumped to their feet, instinctively reaching for weapons. The front window had been smashed in, and dark-clad figures were already storming the room.

"Get down!" Elena shouted, grabbing the nearest object for cover as bullets tore through the air.

Amelia ducked behind the couch; her laptop still open on the coffee table. "We need to protect the files!" she yelled.

Olivia was already firing back, her face set with determination. "There's too many of them!"

Isabella was by the door, trying to block the entry as more men pushed their way inside. "We're not going to hold them off for long!"

Suddenly, Mikhail and Alexei burst back into the room, guns drawn. "We need to fall back!" Alexei shouted. "There's too many!"

Sophia, who had been crouched in the corner, looked up with wide eyes. She hesitated for a moment, then moved to join the others, but Elena caught her with a questioning glance. Something didn't feel right.

"Sophia, what's going on?" Elena asked, her voice laced

with suspicion.

Sophia's face turned pale, and for a split second, the room seemed to freeze.

Before she could answer, Mikhail's voice cut through the chaos. "She's the traitor, Elena. She's working with Nickolav."

Elena's heart dropped, her mind reeling from the accusation. "What?"

Sophia's face twisted in panic, but she didn't deny it. Instead, she stood frozen, the weight of her guilt evident on her face.

"I didn't have a choice," Sophia whispered, tears welling up in her eyes. "She threatened my family. She said she'd kill them if I didn't help her. I didn't know what else to do."

"You sold us out?" Olivia demanded; her voice filled with betrayal.

Sophia's tears spilled over, her voice shaking. "I didn't want to! I've been trying to protect you all, but... I couldn't risk my family. She was always watching."

Elena's mind was spinning, torn between anger and the realization of Sophia's impossible situation. But there was no time to process it—the attackers were closing in.

Mikhail's voice was cold and hard. "We need to leave her behind. She's a liability."

"No," Elena said firmly. "She's one of us. We're not leaving her."

Before they could argue further, the men outside were breaking through their defences. They had only moments left.

"Grab the files!" Alexei barked, moving to the exit. "We need to get out now!"

In the chaos of gunfire and betrayal, the group fled the

safehouse, escaping through the back alleyways of Moscow. They ran, their breath ragged, their hearts heavy with the weight of what had just transpired.

Sophia, her face streaked with tears, followed silently, knowing that she would never be fully trusted again.

As they disappeared into the night, Nickolav's grip tightened. The group was fractured, and the stakes had never been higher.

But they still had the documents. And as long as they could keep the evidence safe, there was still hope.

The battle was far from over.

Chapter 11:
The Price of Truth

The cold wind of Moscow nipped at their faces as the group moved swiftly through the narrow alleyways, their breaths visible in the dim light of the early morning. Elena led the way, her eyes scanning every corner for signs of danger, her mind racing as she replayed the events of the night before. They had narrowly escaped Nickolav's men, but the cracks within the group were growing deeper. Trust had been shattered, and now, they were running on borrowed time.

Sophia walked behind them, her face pale and tear-streaked, keeping her distance from the others. The weight of her betrayal hung in the air like a heavy fog, suffocating any sense of unity they once had. She had been their friend, their sister in arms, but now… now she was something else. An outcast. A traitor.

"We can't just keep running," Amelia said, her voice breathless as they reached the edge of the city. "We need a plan."

"I'm working on it," Alexei replied, his voice tight with frustration. He glanced back at Sophia, his eyes cold. "But first, we need to figure out what to do with her."

Sophia flinched, knowing the weight of her actions was still fresh in everyone's minds. She had endangered them all, and no amount of apologies could undo that.

"We're not leaving her behind," Elena said firmly, cutting through the tension. "She made a mistake, but she's still one of us."

Olivia looked at Elena, her eyes filled with doubt. "How can you still defend her after what she did? She sold us out to Nickolav. We could've all been killed."

"I know," Elena admitted, her voice softening. "But if we start turning on each other now, Nickolav's already won. We need to stick together if we have any chance of surviving this."

Isabella, who had been silent until now, crossed her arms, her face unreadable. "The truth is, none of us can fully trust her. But Elena's right. If we don't pull together, we're all dead."

Sophia remained silent, her guilt palpable, as they found a temporary hideout in an abandoned warehouse on the outskirts of Moscow. The place was cold and dark, with broken windows and rusting metal beams, but it provided them with much-needed cover from Nickolav's men. For now, it would have to do.

Inside the warehouse, they gathered around a small table, illuminated by the glow of Amelia's laptop. The documents were spread out before them, detailing the full extent of Nickolav's empire—the fraudulent charitable trusts, the insurance scams, the trafficking operations. It was enough to bring her down if they could get the evidence into the right hands.

"We need to send this to the press," Amelia said, her voice steady despite the tension. "Once this hits the news, Nickolav won't be able to hide anymore."

"Agreed," Alexei said, leaning over the table. "But we have

to be careful. If we make one wrong move, she'll find us. And she won't hesitate to kill every last one of us."

As they discussed their plan, Sophia stood off to the side, watching with a heavy heart. She had once been a central part of their mission, but now she felt like an outsider. She wanted to make things right, to prove that she was still on their side, but she knew it wouldn't be that simple.

Suddenly, the sound of footsteps echoed from outside the warehouse. Everyone froze.

"Did anyone follow us?" Olivia whispered, her hand instinctively reaching for her gun.

Alexei shook his head, his eyes narrowing as he moved toward the entrance. "No one should've been able to track us here."

The footsteps grew louder, closer.

"We need to move," Isabella said urgently, grabbing the documents. "Now."

Before they could act, the door to the warehouse was kicked open, and Nickolav's operatives stormed in. Dressed in black and armed to the teeth, they moved with the precision of trained killers, their faces obscured by masks.

"Get down!" Elena yelled, pulling Sophia to the floor just as gunfire erupted.

The group scattered, ducking behind crates and metal beams as bullets flew through the air. Amelia's laptop was knocked to the ground, the screen flickering before going black. The documents they had so desperately tried to protect were now exposed, lying in the open.

"We can't let them get the files!" Alexei shouted, firing back at the attackers. "They'll destroy everything."

Elena's heart raced as she glanced at the scattered papers. They were so close to bringing Nickolav down, but if the operatives got their hands on the evidence, it would all be for nothing. Desperation clawed at her as she made a split-second decision.

"Cover me!" she shouted, running toward the documents.

Olivia and Isabella provided cover fire, their guns blazing as Elena darted across the room. She slid to the ground, grabbing the papers and stuffing them into her bag just as a bullet grazed her arm.

"Elena!" Amelia screamed, but Elena waved her off, gritting her teeth through the pain.

"I'm fine," Elena gasped, clutching her arm as blood seeped through her fingers. "We need to get out of here!"

But the operatives were closing in, their movements swift and deadly. It was clear they were under orders not to leave anyone alive.

Amelia's heart pounded as she looked around, realising that there was no clear way out. They were trapped.

"We're not going to make it," Olivia muttered, her voice filled with despair.

"Don't say that," Elena snapped, her eyes blazing with determination. "We're not giving up."

In that moment, Sophia stood up, her face set with resolve. "I can get us out."

The others looked at her in disbelief.

"You?" Alexei asked, his voice thick with suspicion.

Sophia nodded, her eyes meeting his. "I know Nickolav's men. I know how they operate. I can create a distraction long enough for you to escape."

"How do we know this isn't another trap?" Olivia demanded; her anger barely contained.

"You don't," Sophia admitted, her voice steady. "But you're running out of options. Let me fix this."

For a moment, no one spoke. The gunfire was getting closer, and they all knew they didn't have time to debate.

Elena was the first to speak. "We let her try."

Alexei hesitated, but finally nodded. "Do it."

Sophia took a deep breath, her heart pounding in her chest as she moved toward the operatives. She had been part of their world once, a pawn in Nickolav's game. But now, she was determined to destroy the queen who had manipulated her.

She stepped out into the open, her hands raised in surrender. The operatives hesitated, lowering their guns slightly as they recognized her.

"I'm with you," Sophia called out, her voice strong despite the fear gripping her heart. "I've been working with Nickolav this whole time. Let me help you."

The leader of the group, a tall man with cold eyes, narrowed his gaze. "Why should we believe you?"

Sophia's mind raced. "Because I know where they're hiding the real evidence. The files they have are decoys. If you let me go, I'll take you to the real stash."

For a moment, the man considered her offer, his finger hovering over the trigger. Then, with a nod, he signalled for his men to stand down.

"Lead the way," he said, his voice dripping with suspicion.

As Sophia led them toward the far side of the warehouse,

Elena and the others took their chance. They slipped out the back, moving as quickly and quietly as they could.

Outside, the cold night air hit them like a shock, but they didn't stop running until they were far from the warehouse.

"We made it," Amelia gasped, clutching the bag of documents. "I can't believe we made it."

Elena's eyes were filled with a mixture of relief and sorrow. "Sophia... she sacrificed herself."

"We don't know that yet," Alexei said, though his voice was heavy with doubt.

The group stood in silence; their breath visible in the cold air. They had escaped, but the cost had been high. Trust had been broken, alliances tested, and Sophia... her fate was uncertain.

But they still had the documents. And as long as they held the evidence, they had a chance to bring Nickolav down.

The battle was far from over, but for now, they had won.

Chapter 12:
The Edge of Sacrifice

The dim light of dawn filtered through the cracked windows of their new hideout, a rundown safehouse on the outskirts of Moscow. Dust particles danced in the air, and the silence was thick, broken only by the distant sounds of the city waking up. Inside, the group sat in uneasy silence, each of them processing the events of the last few hours. They had barely escaped Nickolav's operatives, but at what cost?

Elena winced as Amelia bandaged her wounded arm, the pain a sharp reminder of how close they had come to losing everything. The bag of documents sat on the table in front of them, the key to exposing Nickolav's crimes and dismantling her empire once and for all. But without Sophia, everything felt fractured.

"Do you think she made it out alive?" Olivia asked, her voice quiet, almost hopeful.

No one answered. The weight of Sophia's betrayal still hung heavy in the air, but so did the guilt of leaving her behind.

"She knew what she was doing," Alexei said finally, his voice rough. "She made her choice."

Elena stared at the bag of documents, her mind racing. Sophia had been more than a teammate—she had been family.

And now, with her gone, the team was broken. Trust was hard to rebuild, and their mission was growing more dangerous by the second.

"We can't keep focusing on what we lost," Isabella said, her voice firm. "Nickolav is still out there, and she's getting closer every day. We need to move forward."

Amelia nodded in agreement. "Isabella's right. We have everything we need to expose her, but we can't stay here. We need a new plan."

Elena knew they were right, but the ache of Sophia's absence gnawed at her. She couldn't shake the feeling that they were walking into an even bigger trap, and the deeper they went, the higher the stakes became.

"Where do we go next?" Olivia asked, her voice uncertain. "Nickolav has men everywhere. Moscow's not safe."

Alexei stepped forward, pulling out a map of Europe and spreading it across the table. "We'll have to move fast, and we'll need help. There's a journalist in Berlin I trust—Anton Volkov. He's been trying to expose Nickolav for years. If we can get the documents to him, he can get them into the hands of the right people."

"But we'll need to be careful," Isabella added. "Nickolav won't just sit back and let us expose her. She's going to send everything she has to stop us."

Elena nodded, her mind already working through the details. "We need to split up. It'll be harder for her to track all of us if we're in different places. Some of us will head to Berlin to meet with Anton, and the rest will stay behind to create a diversion."

"Are you sure about splitting up?" Amelia asked, concern

etched on her face. "We're stronger together."

"We don't have a choice," Elena said, her voice resolute. "Nickolav's resources are almost limitless. If we stay together, we're a bigger target. But if we split up, we buy ourselves time."

The group exchanged glances; the unease evident. They had been through hell together, but now they were facing a new kind of danger—a danger that threatened to tear them apart from the inside out.

As they prepared for the next leg of their mission, Alexei pulled Elena aside, his face lined with worry.

"Elena, I know you want to save everyone, but you need to think about what this is going to cost us. We're going up against someone who won't stop until we're dead. Are you prepared for that?"

Elena met his gaze, her resolve hardening. "I'm not giving up, Alexei. We've come too far to stop now. Nickolav needs to be exposed, and if that means we have to make sacrifices, then so be it."

Alexei sighed, his shoulders tense. "Just... don't lose yourself in this. We need you."

Elena looked away, her thoughts drifting back to Sophia. Was she already losing herself? The mission had consumed them all, and now they were teetering on the edge, unsure of who they could truly trust.

Later that night, as the group finalised their plans to split up, a soft knock echoed through the safehouse. Everyone tensed, their hands instinctively reaching for their weapons. Alexei moved toward the door; his gun raised.

"Who's there?" he called out, his voice low and dangerous.

"It's me," a familiar voice answered from the other side.

The group exchanged stunned looks before Alexei cautiously opened the door.

There stood Sophia, bruised and exhausted, but very much alive.

"Sophia," Elena breathed, relief washing over her, but it was quickly replaced by wariness. "What happened?"

Sophia stepped inside, her eyes downcast. "I…I escaped. I led them away from you and managed to slip away when they thought they had me cornered."

Olivia's voice was sharp. "And how do we know you're not leading them straight to us again?"

Sophia flinched; the pain of Olivia's words visible on her face. "I'm not here to hurt you. I swear. I just want to make things right."

Isabella crossed her arms, her expression unreadable. "You betrayed us once, Sophia. Why should we trust you now?"

Tears welled up in Sophia's eyes, but she stood her ground. "I know I messed up, and I'll spend the rest of my life trying to make up for it. But I'm still one of you. We all want the same thing—to stop Nickolav. Please… let me help."

The room fell into tense silence as everyone weighed their options. Trusting Sophia again was a risk, but they were running out of time and options.

Elena was the first to break the silence. "We need every ally we can get. If Sophia's willing to fight with us, then I say we give her a chance."

Amelia nodded, though her expression remained cautious. "But we'll be watching her closely. One wrong move, and she's out. For good."

Sophia nodded, her face a mixture of gratitude and sorrow. "I understand."

As the night wore on, the group finalised their plans. Elena, Alexei, and Olivia would head to Berlin to meet Anton Volkov, while Amelia, Isabella, and Sophia would stay behind to create a diversion, buying them time to deliver the documents.

But as they prepared to part ways, the weight of their mission pressed down on them all. Nickolav was closing in, and the cost of failure was higher than ever. They were running out of time, and soon, they would have to face the ultimate question: how far were they willing to go to stop Nickolav—and what price were they willing to pay?

Chapter 13:
Shadows of Betrayal

The streets of Moscow were eerily quiet in the early morning light as Elena, Alexei, and Olivia prepared to make their way to Berlin. Every step felt heavy, weighed down by the tension of their mission and the uncertainty that lay ahead. They had the documents—the incriminating evidence that could take down Nickolav—but their path was fraught with danger, and each moment seemed to draw Nickolav's operatives closer.

Inside the safehouse, the group gathered around a small table, going over the final details of their plan. The room was dimly lit, casting long shadows on the faces of those who had grown accustomed to the weight of fear.

Mikhail, one of their closest allies since arriving in Moscow, stood apart from the group. His face was stern, his expression unreadable as he watched them prepare to leave. Elena couldn't help but notice the way his gaze lingered on Alexei, a quiet intensity in his eyes. Something was bothering him.

"I'm sorry," Mikhail said abruptly, breaking the silence. His voice was low, and there was a strange finality to it. "But this is where I take my leave."

Everyone froze, turning to face him.

"What do you mean?" Olivia asked, her voice tinged with

confusion.

Mikhail looked at each of them in turn, his expression somber. "I've done everything I can for you here in Moscow. But now, I need to go underground. Nickolav's reach is growing, and I can't risk being captured. You all have a fighting chance, but I need to protect myself and the people I care about."

Elena exchanged a glance with Alexei. Mikhail had been their lifeline in Moscow, helping them evade Nickolav's men and providing them with crucial intel. But now, as the stakes grew higher, it seemed he was pulling back, retreating into the shadows.

"We understand," Elena said finally, her voice steady. "You've helped us more than we can ever repay, Mikhail."

He nodded, his eyes softening slightly. "Just make sure you finish what you started. Nickolav needs to be stopped."

With that, Mikhail turned and walked toward the door, his steps echoing in the silence. He didn't look back as he disappeared into the Moscow morning, leaving the group to face the dangers ahead without him.

As the remaining team split into two groups, Elena, Alexei, and Olivia boarded the first train out of Moscow, heading toward Berlin. The tension inside the train was palpable as they sat in silence, each of them lost in their thoughts. The documents, safely tucked inside Alexei's bag, felt heavier than ever, as if they carried not only the weight of evidence but also the burden of their mission.

"Who exactly is Anton Volkov?" Olivia asked after a long stretch of silence, breaking through the haze of tension. "What makes him so important?"

Elena leaned back in her seat; her gaze distant as she thought back to the first time she'd heard Anton's name. "He's a journalist—a very good one. He's been investigating Nickolav for years, trying to expose her empire. But she's always been one step ahead of him. He knows the ins and outs of her operations better than almost anyone. If we can get the documents to him, he'll know how to get them to the right people—people who can bring Nickolav down."

Alexei nodded; his jaw clenched. "Anton's been trying to take her down from the outside for a long time. We're hoping that with these documents, he'll finally have enough evidence to make it happen."

Olivia frowned. "And you trust him? He's not going to turn on us?"

Elena hesitated. "I trust that he hates Nickolav as much as we do. That's all we can rely on right now."

The train rumbled along the tracks, carrying them closer to Berlin, and with each passing hour, the sense of unease grew. They were leaving behind the relative safety of Moscow, heading straight into the lion's den. Nickolav's operatives would no doubt be waiting for them, and the closer they got to Berlin, the more dangerous their mission became.

Meanwhile, back in Moscow, Amelia, Isabella, and Sophia were preparing their diversion. Their part of the plan was risky, but it was necessary to buy Elena and the others enough time to reach Anton and hand over the documents.

Sophia moved through the safehouse with a quiet intensity, her every action deliberate. Amelia and Isabella watched her closely, still unsure if they could fully trust her after everything that had happened. Her betrayal had left scars that were slow to heal, but they needed her now more than ever.

"Are you sure you're up for this?" Isabella asked, her tone laced with caution.

Sophia looked at her, her eyes shadowed with guilt but filled with resolve. "I'm ready. I know what I have to do."

Amelia crossed her arms, leaning against the wall. "Just remember, this only works if we stay one step ahead of Nickolav's men. If they catch us, it's over."

Sophia nodded; her expression grim. "I won't let that happen."

As night fell, Elena, Alexei, and Olivia arrived in Berlin, their hearts pounding with the weight of what lay ahead. The city felt foreign, the air thick with tension. They made their way through the streets, moving cautiously as they approached their meeting point with Anton Volkov.

Anton's reputation preceded him—he was known for his fearless reporting, his relentless pursuit of the truth. But he was also a man of shadows, always one step ahead of those he sought to expose. Meeting with him meant stepping deeper into the dangerous world of underground journalism, where information was as valuable as gold, and betrayal was always a possibility.

As they approached the agreed-upon location—a small, nondescript café tucked away in a quiet Berlin alley—Elena's nerves were on high alert. They had everything riding on this meeting. Anton Volkov was their last hope.

Inside, the café was dimly lit, the air thick with the smell of coffee and cigarette smoke. At a table in the corner, a man in his late thirties sat alone, his sharp blue eyes scanning the room with practiced precision. His dark hair was slightly tousled, and his face was a mask of quiet determination.

"That's him," Alexei muttered under his breath.

Elena took a deep breath, steeling herself as they approached Anton. This was it—the moment they had been preparing for. If Anton could get the documents into the right hands, they might finally have a chance to take down Nickolav once and for all.

Anton looked up as they reached his table, his gaze flicking over them with cold appraisal. "You must be Elena," he said, his voice low and smooth. "Alexei told me you'd be coming."

Elena nodded, her heart racing. "We have what you need. Everything to bring Nickolav down."

Anton's eyes gleamed with interest as he motioned for them to sit. "Good. Let's see what you've got."

But as they sat down, a chill ran down Elena's spine. The world of shadows they were entering was fraught with danger, and the closer they got to the truth, the more they risked losing everything.

Chapter 14:
Shattered Lives

Anton sat in the dim light of the café; the documents spread across the table like a grim tapestry of Nickolav's many sins. His fingers traced the edges of the papers, his face a mask of cold intensity as he examined the damning evidence in front of him. For the first time in years, he had what he needed to expose her, but the road ahead was far more dangerous than any of them could imagine.

Elena, Alexei, and Olivia watched him in tense silence, each of them aware that they were walking on the razor's edge. The betrayal Sophia had committed still hung in the air like a spectre, and the team's fragile unity was already strained. Every second felt like a countdown to disaster.

Anton's eyes flicked up from the documents, meeting Elena's gaze with an intensity that made her stomach churn. "This is… more than I expected," he said quietly, his voice tinged with both awe and dread. "Nickolav's crimes run deeper than I realized. But there's something else I need you to understand."

He leaned back in his chair, his expression darkening. "A few years ago, I met an elderly couple—a husband and wife— who had lost everything to one of Nickolav's schemes. They were promised security in their old age, a charitable trust that would take care of them as they retired. It was supposed to be their safety net, a lifeline for when they couldn't support themselves anymore."

Elena leaned in closer, sensing that this story was about to reveal more than just another one of Nickolav's deceptions. She could see the pain etched in Anton's face, and the way he spoke made it clear that this memory haunted him.

"The husband, Viktor, was a retired factory worker, and his wife, Marina, had spent her life taking care of their children. They were simple people—trusting, kind-hearted. They didn't deserve what happened to them," Anton continued, his voice growing harder. "They invested everything they had in Nickolav's so-called trust, believing it would provide for them. But it was all a lie. They lost everything. Their home, their savings, their dignity…"

Anton's gaze drifted to the window, where the Berlin streets were beginning to darken with the onset of night. "Viktor had a heart attack the day he found out. The stress, the fear—it was too much for him. He died on the spot. And Marina… she couldn't bear the grief. She fell into a coma shortly after his death, and she's been in that state ever since."

A heavy silence fell over the group, the weight of Anton's words sinking in. Elena's throat tightened. It wasn't just the criminal empire they were trying to take down—it was the devastation Nickolav had wrought on innocent people, people who had trusted her and had their lives destroyed in return.

"Do you know how many more people like Viktor and Marina are out there?" Olivia asked quietly, her voice filled with sorrow.

Anton shook his head slowly, a bitter edge to his tone. "I don't. That's the worst part. I don't know how many families have been torn apart, how many lives have been ruined by her schemes. I don't know how many husbands, wives, children…

have lost someone they loved because of Nickolav's greed. And I don't think we'll ever truly know the full extent of the damage she caused."

Elena clenched her fists under the table, anger simmering inside her. It wasn't just about exposing Nickolav anymore—it was about justice. For Viktor, for Marina, and for all the others who had been victims of her cruelty. But with every passing moment, the stakes grew higher, and Elena knew they were running out of time.

Alexei, who had been uncharacteristically silent throughout Anton's story, finally spoke, his voice heavy with a burden he had carried for too long. "There's a reason I've stuck with you, with all of this," he said, looking directly at Elena. "I didn't just show up at Erica's wedding by coincidence. I came because I knew the sisterhood—your sisterhood—was the only group capable of taking down someone like Nickolav."

Elena's brow furrowed as Alexei continued. "I've been watching Nickolav for years, trying to gather enough evidence to expose her. But I knew I couldn't do it alone. She's too powerful, too well-connected. And then… I saw all of you."

He glanced around at the group, his eyes lingering on each one of them. "I saw how you worked together, how you had this unbreakable bond. And I knew you were the ones who could do it. Nickolav has a way of manipulating everyone around her, of getting people to trust her just enough so that she can destroy them. But not you. Not the sisterhood."

Elena felt a strange mix of emotions welling up inside her— surprise, pride, and a sense of responsibility. She had always known their bond was special, but to hear Alexei say it, to hear that he had been watching them, believing in them, was something she hadn't expected.

"You knew about sisterhood from the beginning?" Olivia

asked, her voice sharp with suspicion.

Alexei nodded. "I knew that if anyone could expose Nickolav for what she really is, it was you five. That's why I approached you at Erica's wedding. I needed help, but more importantly, I needed your help. And I still do."

Elena exchanged a glance with Olivia and Alexei, feeling the weight of the truth settle over her. It wasn't just about Nickolav anymore. It was about the people she had hurt, the lives she had destroyed. And now, with Anton on their side, they had a chance—perhaps their only chance—to bring her down for good.

But as Anton finished examining the documents, a cold sense of dread filled the room. Outside, the shadows seemed to lengthen, and Elena's instincts screamed that something was wrong.

Suddenly, Anton's phone buzzed on the table. He glanced at it, his expression darkening as he read the message.

"They're here," he muttered.

Before anyone could react, the doors to the café burst open, and Nickolav's men stormed in, guns drawn and eyes cold with intent. Elena's heart raced, her mind spinning as chaos erupted around them.

Anton jumped to his feet, grabbing the documents and shoving them into his coat. "We need to move. Now!" he shouted.

As bullets flew, the group scrambled to escape, but Elena knew one thing for certain: someone had betrayed them. Someone within their ranks had tipped Nickolav off, and now they were in more danger than ever.

Chapter 15:
Broken Trust

The café exploded into chaos as bullets ripped through the air. Tables overturned, glass shattered, and screams echoed in the confined space. Elena's heart pounded in her chest as she dove behind an upturned table, her breath coming in ragged gasps. Alexei was beside her, his eyes scanning the room for an exit, while Olivia crouched a few feet away, her hand trembling as she clutched her phone. Anton had already bolted, the incriminating documents tucked under his coat.

"How did they find us?" Olivia shouted over the gunfire, panic edging her voice.

Elena didn't answer. She couldn't. Her mind was racing, trying to process how everything had gone wrong so quickly. They had been so careful, so precise. Yet somehow, Nickolav's men had known exactly where to find them. Someone had tipped them off.

Anton reappeared at the back entrance, signaling for them to move. "We've got to get out of here!" he barked, his voice cutting through the din.

Elena glanced at Olivia and Alexei, her pulse hammering in her ears. They had no choice but to trust Anton, at least for now. With one last look around the room, she made a dash for the exit, feeling the heat of a bullet graze her arm as she moved.

They spilled into the alley behind the café, panting and wide-eyed, the adrenaline surging through their veins. But the sense of relief was short-lived. The realization hit all at once—someone among them had betrayed them. Someone had led Nickolav's men straight to them, and now their entire mission was at risk.

Elena pressed her back against the alley wall, trying to steady her breathing. "Who was it?" she demanded; her voice sharp with accusation. "Who told them where we were?"

Anton, still clutching the documents, looked equally shaken. "It wasn't me," he said, his tone defensive. "I didn't tell anyone about our meeting."

"How do we know that?" Alexei shot back, his eyes narrowing. "For all we know, you could've been working with Nickolav from the start."

"Don't be ridiculous," Anton snapped, his voice rising in frustration. "Why would I risk my life for these documents if I was working with her? I'm trying to expose her, not protect her."

Olivia stepped forward, her face pale. "Then who? If it wasn't you, and it wasn't Anton…"

A heavy silence settled over the group. The air was thick with suspicion, the unspoken question hanging between them. "Who betrayed us?"

Elena's mind raced through the possibilities. Anton had the most to gain by betraying them, but his fear seemed genuine. Alexei had been with them for months now, but could he really be trusted? And Olivia—hadn't she been acting strangely ever since Sophia's betrayal?

"Someone told them where we were," Elena said coldly. "And we're not leaving this alley until we figure out who."

Olivia's eyes darted nervously between Elena and Alexei. "You're not seriously suggesting it was one of us, are you?"

Elena took a step closer, her voice dangerously calm. "It has to be. No one else knew about the meeting. We were careful, Olivia. We've been careful from the start."

Alexei folded his arms, his jaw clenched in frustration. "We don't have time for this. Nickolav's operatives are probably sweeping the city as we speak. We need to figure out our next move before they catch up to us."

Anton nodded, though his expression was grim. "Alexei's right. Arguing over this now won't help us. We need to keep moving."

But Elena wasn't ready to let it go. She couldn't. Not when the traitor was still standing among them, waiting for the next opportunity to strike.

Her eyes flicked to Olivia. The quiet, nervous girl who had been with them from the beginning. The girl who had been by Sophia's side when she had betrayed them, who had watched as the team's trust crumbled around them. Was she hiding something?

"Olivia," Elena said slowly, her voice low. "Where were you right before the meeting?"

Olivia blinked, caught off guard by the question. "What? I—I was with you, Elena. We were together the whole time."

"No, we weren't," Elena pressed. "You went to the bathroom before we left the safehouse. You were gone for a while. What were you doing?"

The color drained from Olivia's face. "I… I wasn't doing anything! I swear! I just needed a minute to myself. You know how stressful all of this has been—"

"Save it," Alexei interrupted, stepping forward. His eyes

were hard, his voice laced with anger. "This isn't just about stress, Olivia. Someone called Nickolav's men. Someone put us all in danger."

"I didn't do it!" Olivia cried, her voice cracking with desperation. "I would never—"

"Enough!" Elena shouted, silencing the argument. She could feel the cracks forming in their already fragile alliance, and she knew that if they didn't find the traitor soon, the entire mission would fall apart.

"We don't have time for this," Anton said again, his voice more insistent now. "We need to get somewhere safe. We'll deal with the traitor later."

Elena reluctantly nodded, though her mind was still racing. She couldn't shake the feeling that something was off, that they were missing a crucial piece of the puzzle. But with Nickolav's men closing in, they had no choice but to keep moving.

The group made their way through the darkened streets of Berlin, their footsteps echoing in the empty alleyways. Every corner felt like a potential trap, every shadow a hidden enemy. They needed to find safety, but where could they go when they couldn't trust each other?

As they reached a quiet, abandoned warehouse on the outskirts of the city, Anton led them inside. The building was cold and empty, its walls covered in graffiti and its floors strewn with debris. It wasn't much, but it was a place to regroup.

Once inside, Anton sat down and pulled the documents from his coat, spreading them out on the floor in front of him. "We need to keep moving forward," he said, his voice firm. "Nickolav knows we're onto her now, but these documents are the key to taking her down. We just need to figure out our next move."

Elena knelt beside him, her eyes scanning the papers, but her mind was still on the traitor. She couldn't focus, not when she didn't know who to trust anymore.

"We should split up," Alexei suggested, pacing the room. "Cover more ground, throw Nickolav's men off our trail. Maybe then we can figure out who's been feeding her information."

"No," Elena said firmly. "We stick together. Splitting up just gives the traitor more opportunities to sabotage us."

Alexei stopped pacing, his eyes meeting hers. "And what happens when Nickolav's men find us again, Elena? We can't keep running forever."

Elena's jaw tightened. "We'll figure it out. But we're not splitting up."

Anton sighed, rubbing his temples. "We don't have time for this. We need to make a decision—now."

Before Elena could respond, the door to the warehouse creaked open, and the sound of footsteps echoed through the empty space.

They froze, every muscle tense as they waited for the intruder to reveal themselves.

A shadowy figure stepped into the dim light, their face hidden by the hood of their jacket. Elena's heart pounded in her chest as the figure moved closer, their steps slow and deliberate.

When the figure finally lowered their hood, a familiar face emerged—Sophia.

Her eyes were cold, her expression unreadable. "I think I might have some answers," she said quietly, her voice laced with the kind of calm that only came before a storm.

Chapter 16:
The Final Reckoning

The warehouse fell into a suffocating silence as Sophia stepped into the dim light, her face a mask of cold determination. Elena's heart pounded in her chest, torn between shock and fury. The last time they had seen Sophia, she had betrayed them, handing over critical information to Nickolav. Now, here she was again, walking back into their lives as if she hadn't left them to die.

Alexei's hand tightened around the grip of his gun; his eyes narrowed in suspicion. "What are you doing here, Sophia?" His voice was tense, barely concealing the rage simmering beneath the surface.

Sophia didn't flinch. "I'm here to finish what we started. But first, you need to hear me out."

Elena stepped forward, unable to contain the storm of emotions swirling inside her. "Hear you out? After what you did to us? You handed us over to Nickolav! We trusted you, and you sold us out!"

Sophia's jaw clenched, her eyes flashing with frustration. "I didn't betray you. I made a deal with Nickolav to protect you—all of you. She was going to kill you that night. I had no choice."

"You expect us to believe that?" Alexei scoffed, his voice

dripping with sarcasm. "You were working with her the whole time!"

"No," Sophia shot back, her voice fierce. "I was trying to protect you. I had to make it look like I was on her side to buy us time, to figure out her next move. If I hadn't done what I did, none of you would be standing here right now."

Elena's mind reeled. Could Sophia be telling the truth? It was hard to trust anything she said after everything that had happened, but there was a conviction in her voice that made Elena pause. Still, the betrayal cut deep, and the wound wasn't something that could be healed easily.

"We don't have time for this," Anton interrupted, his voice firm but urgent. He was still clutching the documents they had risked everything to obtain. "Nickolav's men are closing in. If we're going to make our move, it has to be now."

Sophia nodded, her gaze shifting from Elena to Anton. "That's why I'm here. I have something that can help us. I know where Nickolav is keeping her most dangerous assets—documents, ledgers, everything. If we expose her, we can bring her entire empire down. But we need to act fast."

Alexei shook his head, disbelief still clouding his judgment. "And we're just supposed to trust you now? After everything?"

Sophia looked him square in the eye. "You don't have to trust me. But you know that what I'm saying is true. Nickolav is a monster, and if we don't stop her now, none of us will get out of this alive."

Elena's heart raced as the weight of the decision pressed down on her. Time was running out. They were backed into a corner with no easy way out. The trust among them was shattered, and yet, they had no choice but to take a risk—because if Sophia was right, this was their last chance to stop Nickolav once and for all.

Elena turned to the group, her voice steady despite the fear clawing at her insides. "We have to decide, right now. Do we trust her, or do we go our separate ways and risk everything falling apart?"

The silence that followed was agonising. Alexei, Anton, Olivia—they all looked at each other, uncertainty and fear reflected in their eyes. But there was no time left for doubt. Nickolav's men were closing in, and the fate of everything they had fought for hung in the balance.

"I say we go for it," Anton said finally, his voice filled with resolve. "This is our best shot at bringing her down."

Alexei hesitated, his eyes flicking between Sophia and Elena. Finally, he nodded, though the distrust still lingered in his gaze. "Fine. But if this is another one of your tricks, Sophia, I won't hesitate."

Sophia's lips pressed into a thin line. "I wouldn't expect you to."

The plan was hastily put together as they made their way to the heart of Nickolav's empire—a sprawling, heavily guarded estate on the outskirts of the city. The air was thick with tension, every step feeling like it could be their last. As they approached, Elena's mind raced with a thousand possibilities. What if this was all a trap? What if Sophia had been playing them from the start?

But there was no turning back now. The estate loomed ahead, its high walls and guarded towers casting ominous shadows in the night. They crept along the perimeter, using the darkness as cover, until they reached a narrow entrance that Sophia had scouted earlier.

Inside, the air was heavy with the scent of wealth and power, but beneath it, Elena could sense the rot of corruption. This was the heart of Nickolav's empire, the place where she had built her fortune on the suffering of others.

Sophia led them through a maze of hallways, her movements swift and precise. She seemed to know the layout well, and for a moment, Elena wondered just how deeply Sophia had been embedded in Nickolav's operation. But now wasn't the time for questions.

As they reached a large, secure room at the center of the estate, Sophia stopped, her hand hovering over a panel on the wall. "This is it," she whispered. "Nickolav keeps her most important documents here. Once we get them, it's over for her."

Anton stepped forward, his eyes scanning the panel. "Can you open it?"

Sophia nodded, quickly inputting a series of codes. The door hissed open, revealing a vault filled with files, ledgers, and stacks of cash. Anton immediately began sorting through the papers, his hands moving with the practiced efficiency of someone who had been chasing this for far too long.

But just as they started loading the documents into bags, the sound of footsteps echoed down the hall.

"They're coming," Alexei hissed, drawing his gun.

Elena's heart raced as they quickly prepared for a showdown. They had the evidence they needed, but now they had to escape with it—and Nickolav wouldn't let them leave without a fight.

The door burst open, and Nickolav herself stood in the doorway, flanked by armed men. Her eyes were cold, calculating, as she took in the scene before her. "I knew you'd come for me eventually," she said, her voice dripping with disdain. "But did you really think you could win?"

Elena's pulse quickened as she met Nickolav's gaze. "We have everything we need to expose you."

Nickolav's lips curled into a smile. "Do you really think the world cares about your little crusade? People like me don't fall because of a few documents. I built this empire on blood, and it will take more than you to tear it down."

Sophia stepped forward, her eyes blazing with fury. "You've hurt too many people, Nickolav. It ends tonight."

Nickolav's smile faded, her eyes narrowing. "You always were too sentimental, Sophia. That's why you were never fit for this world."

With a snap of her fingers, her men raised their weapons. The room exploded into chaos.

Elena dove behind a desk, bullets flying overhead as the battle raged. Alexei returned fire, while Anton frantically gathered the remaining documents. Olivia stayed low, her eyes wide with terror as she clutched her bag of evidence.

In the middle of the chaos, Elena saw Nickolav retreating toward the back of the room. She couldn't let her escape. Without hesitation, Elena sprinted forward, her heart pounding as she closed the distance between them.

Nickolav turned, her face twisted with rage as she drew a knife. "You think you can stop me?" she snarled, lunging at Elena.

But Elena was ready. With a swift movement, she disarmed Nickolav, sending the knife clattering to the floor. The two women struggled, their movements frantic and desperate, but Elena had the upper hand. With one final push, she knocked

Nickolav to the ground, pinning her down.

"It's over," Elena spat, her voice cold and resolute.

Nickolav glared up at her, defiant to the end. "This isn't over," she hissed. "It will never be over."

But Elena knew better. With Nickolav subdued and the evidence in hand, they had won.

For now.

Chapter 17:
The Fall of Queen Nickolav

The city of Mumbai was waking up to a new dawn, but for Elena, Isabella, Sophia, Amelia, and Olivia, the night had been endless. After the intense confrontation with Queen Nickolav, they had managed to escape the estate with the incriminating evidence in hand. Anton, alongside Alexei, had spent hours sorting through the mountain of documents, making sure every damning piece of information would be impossible to refute.

Now, they sat in a small, dimly lit room in a safe house, waiting for the world to change.

Sophia paced the floor, her hands trembling slightly from the adrenaline. "It's done," she said, her voice low. "We've sent the evidence to every major news outlet. Nickolav won't be able to run from this."

Elena leaned against the wall, watching the screen of the laptop as the emails went out one by one. "It feels unreal," she admitted. "After everything we've been through, it's finally over."

Anton, who had been silently working at the computer, looked up. "Not quite. Once the news breaks, she'll know we're behind this. She's still dangerous until the police move in."

Sophia stopped pacing, her eyes flicking to the clock. "The

media will have everything in less than an hour. By then, Nickolav's empire will start crumbling from the inside. People will turn on her. No one is loyal to someone who's about to fall."

Amelia, sitting quietly in the corner, spoke up for the first time. "What if she tries to run? We know she has connections—she could disappear."

Anton shook his head. "Not with the kind of evidence we have. This isn't just about her illegal activities. These documents show every bribe, every corrupt official, every person in her pocket. The system that protected her is going to collapse too. There's nowhere for her to hide."

The weight of his words settled over them, filling the room with a tense anticipation. They had exposed Nickolav's empire for what it truly was—a network built on exploitation, greed, and violence. It wasn't just about bringing down a criminal; they were dismantling a system of power.

As dawn broke, the first wave of news hit the media. Headlines screamed across screens:

"Nickolav's Empire Exposed: Dark Secrets of Charity Fraud and Human Trafficking Revealed!"

"Queenpin of Crime: Inside the Collapse of Mumbai's Most Notorious Syndicate"

"Authorities Move to Arrest Nickolav as Evidence Surfaces of Decades-Long Crime Spree"

The news spread like wildfire. Major networks, social media, and even local outlets picked up the story. Journalists dissected the documents, laying out the horrifying details of Nickolav's scams, the trafficking of young girls, and the exploitation of the elderly through fraudulent charitable trusts. The world was finally seeing the full extent of her cruelty.

In the heart of Mumbai, people watched in shock as the story unfolded. Families who had been victims of her scams, like the elderly couple Anton had met, finally saw justice being served. The old man who had died of a heart attack after losing everything was no longer just another victim of an invisible force. His story—and those of countless others—was now known to the world.

It wasn't long before the police moved in.

Nickolav had been holed up in her lavish estate, surrounded by a small group of loyal guards. But no amount of security could protect her from the truth. As the sun climbed higher in the sky, sirens echoed through the streets, cutting through the quiet of the morning.

From their safe house, the group watched as live footage of the raid played across the screen. Dozens of officers swarmed the estate, breaking down the gates and moving in with tactical precision. Nickolav's guards were no match for them; they surrendered almost immediately.

Then, finally, Nickolav appeared.

She was escorted out in handcuffs, her face twisted with fury and defiance. Gone was the woman who once controlled an empire with an iron fist. Now, she was just a criminal, exposed and powerless in the face of justice.

"That's it," Alexei whispered, his voice heavy with emotion. "It's really over."

Elena stared at the screen, her heart pounding. She had dreamed of this moment for so long, and now that it was here, it felt almost surreal. The nightmare that had haunted them all—the phone calls, the threats, the danger—was finally coming to an end.

Amelia leaned against the window, watching the sky turn a brilliant shade of blue. "It's hard to believe," she said quietly. "She's been in control for so long. It's strange to think it's really over."

Olivia, sitting next to her, nodded. "But it's not just her. It's everything she stood for. All the lives she destroyed. Now the world knows."

Later that day, as the dust began to settle, the group gathered one last time. They had spent weeks living in constant fear, fighting for justice in a world that seemed stacked against them. Now, with Nickolav's empire crumbling and her power stripped away, they could finally breathe again.

But the victory was bittersweet.

"So, what now?" Elena asked, her voice heavy with exhaustion. "What happens next?"

Sophia, who had been quiet since the arrest, looked around at her friends. "We move on. We rebuilt. We've won this fight, but there's always more to do. We've seen what people like Nickolav can do when they're unchecked. We can't let that happen again."

Anton nodded in agreement. "The evidence we uncovered— it's only the beginning. We've exposed one monster, but there are more out there. Corruption runs deep, and it won't disappear overnight."

Elena smiled faintly, though there was a deep sadness in her eyes. "We've come so far. It feels like the end of one chapter, but I guess we're just getting started."

The group fell into a comfortable silence, each of them lost in their own thoughts. They had come together through tragedy and betrayal, but in the end, they had triumphed. The cost had been high, but they had made a difference.

Outside, the city of Mumbai bustled with life, unaware of the battles fought in the shadows. But for Elena, Isabella, Sophia, Amelia, and Olivia, the world had changed forever.

And somewhere in the distance, the echoes of Nickolav's empire crumbled into dust.

Chapter 18:
A New Dawn

The victory over Nickolav had shaken the world, but for Elena, Isabella, Sophia, Amelia, and Olivia, it was time to turn a new page. They had brought down a criminal empire and exposed the truth to the world, yet the cost had been high. The journey had left deep scars on all of them—both physically and emotionally. Now, they stood on the edge of a new life, wondering what came next.

The safehouse that had served as their base during the final days of the mission was quiet now. The tension that had once hung in the air had dissipated, replaced by a strange sense of peace. After weeks of danger and uncertainty, they had finally achieved what they set out to do.

Elena, standing on the balcony, looked out over the bustling streets of Mumbai. The city moved on, unaware of the battles fought in its shadows. The world had changed, and so had she. Her phone buzzed with a text—Alexei and Mikhail were on their way.

Inside, the rest of the group gathered around the living room. Sophia, still adjusting to her return to the fold, sat quietly on the couch, watching as Olivia and Amelia laughed over some old memory. Isabella leaned against the doorframe, smiling softly at her friends. Despite everything, they had come back together, their sisterhood stronger than before.

There had been moments when it seemed like they would break—betrayal, fear, and doubt had threatened to tear them apart. But they had weathered the storm, and now, as they faced the future, they did so together.

Elena stepped inside, closing the balcony door behind her. "They're almost here," she announced, her smile widening.

"Finally," Amelia grinned. "It's about time we had a proper reunion."

Half an hour later, the door swung open, and Alexei walked in, followed by Mikhail. The room erupted into cheers and laughter as they embraced, their faces lit with relief and joy. It felt like the closing of a chapter—a moment they had all been waiting for.

Alexei smiled at Elena, his eyes soft with gratitude. "We did it," he said, his voice low. "We really did it."

Elena nodded, her heartfull. "We did. And now, we can finally move on."

Mikhail, who had been quieter than usual, finally spoke up. "You all saved the world. Or at least a part of it." He chuckled, shaking his head. "Not bad for a group of college girls."

"Hey!" Isabella teased, playfully punching him on the arm. "We had some help along the way."

As the laughter settled, the group gathered around the small table in the center of the room. For the first time in what felt like forever, there were no plans to make, no dangers lurking around the corner. They could just be themselves—friends, sisters, allies.

The conversation flowed easily, filled with stories of their mission, the moments of triumph and terror, and the bonds that had been strengthened along the way. But as the evening wore on, talk turned to the future.

"What now?" Sophia asked, her voice tentative. "What happens to us?"

Elena looked around at her friends, her heart swelling with affection for each of them. They had come so far together, but their paths were starting to diverge. "I think we all need some time to figure that out," she admitted. "We've been through a lot, and we deserve a chance to heal, to live."

Olivia nodded. "I'm thinking of going back to school. I've missed normal life—if that's even a thing for us anymore."

Amelia smiled. "I've got some family in Europe. Maybe it's time for a visit."

Isabella leaned back in her chair, her eyes twinkling. "I think I want to stay in Mumbai for a while. This city has become home."

"And what about you, Sophia?" Elena asked, her tone soft.

Sophia hesitated for a moment, then smiled. "I think I'll stay too. I have a lot to make up for, and I want to prove that I'm still part of this team."

The group exchanged glances, their unspoken agreement clear. Despite everything, they were still a family—a sisterhood that had endured through every challenge.

Days turned into weeks, and the world moved on. Nickolav's empire crumbled, and with it, the darkness she had cast over so many lives. The group scattered, each finding their own path forward, but they remained connected, their bond unbreakable.

Elena, Isabella, Amelia, Sophia, and Olivia often met up in Mumbai, their laughter filling the air as they recounted old stories and made new memories. Alexei and Mikhail visited frequently, becoming part of their extended family.

Time passed, but the memories of their mission—the victories, the losses, the sacrifices—remained with them. They had faced the worst, and in doing so, they had found something rare and precious: a family forged in the fires of adversity.

On a warm evening months later, they gathered once again, this time for a quiet dinner on the rooftop of a small restaurant in Mumbai. The stars twinkled above them, the city humming with life below. As they ate, laughed, and reminisced, there was a sense of contentment that settled over them.

"I guess this is our 'happily ever after,'" Olivia said with a smile, raising her glass.

"More like 'happily ever after… for now,'" Amelia corrected, grinning. "Who knows what the future holds?"

"Whatever it is," Elena said, looking around at the faces of those she loved, "we'll face it together."

They clinked their glasses, their laughter ringing out into the night. And for the first time in a long time, they allowed themselves to believe that the worst was behind them. They had fought, they had won, and now they could live.

***

www.ingramcontent.com/pod-product-compliance
Lightning Source LLC
LaVergne TN
LVHW041727190726
843493LV00007B/2240